The
Horoscope Cook Book

SONIA ALLISON

The
Horoscope Cook Book

DECORATED WITH THE SIGNS OF THE ZODIAC

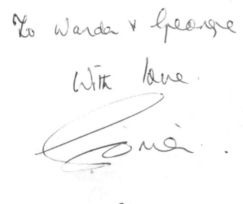

To Wanda & George

With love.

Sonia

December 1971.

London : J. M. Dent & Sons Ltd

First published 1971

© Sonia Allison 1971

Made in Great Britain
at the
Aldine Press · Letchworth · Herts
for
J. M. DENT & SONS LTD
Aldine House · Bedford Street · London

ISBN 0 460 03966 0

To my son Simon

METRIC CONVERSION TABLES

			Exact metric
Working Weight			
400 grammes	=	1 lb.	453.60 gm
200 grammes	=	8 oz.	226.89 gm
100 grammes	=	4 oz.	113.49 gm
50 grammes	=	2 oz.	56.70 gm
25 grammes	=	1 oz.	28.35 gm

ALTERNATIVELY

1 lb. (16 oz.)	=	454 grammes
½ lb. (8 oz.)	=	227 ,,
¼ lb. (4 oz.)	=	113 ,,
2 oz.	=	57 ,,
1 oz.	=	28 ,,
½ oz.	=	14 ,,
¼ oz.	=	7 ,,

Capacity

1 Imperial pint	=	568 millilitres	=	20 fluid oz.	
½ ,, ,,	=	284 ,,	=	10 ,, ,,	
¼ ,, ,,	=	142 ,,	=	5 ,, ,,	(1 gill)
⅛ ,, ,,	=	71 ,,	=	2½ ,, ,,	(4 tablespoons)

ALTERNATIVELY

1 litre	=	992.25 ml	=	35 fluid oz.	=	1¾ pints
½ ,,	=	497.62 ml	=	17½ ,, ,,	=	17½ fluid oz.
¼ ,,	=	248.81 ml	=	8¾ ,, ,,	=	8¾ ,, ,,
⅛ ,,	=	124.40 ml	=	4⅜ ,, ,,	=	7 tablespoons

American Capacity

1 U.S. pint	=	474 ml	=	16 fluid oz.	
½ ,, ,,	=	237 ml	=	8 ,, ,,	(U.S. standard cup)
¼ ,, ,,	=	119 ml	=	4 ,, ,,	(approx. 6 tablespoons)

Contents

CONTENTS

Introduction

MY FIRST contact with 'the stars' began at a very early age. A horoscope was cast for me when I was three years old and was promptly mislaid for the next twenty! When I eventually found it, buried in a large trunk beneath a pile of my late grandmother's 1920 dresses, I was staggered to see how accurate it was and realized that the stars do have a tale to tell if one is prepared to forget one's scepticism and listen.

I must add here that I'm not an astrologer. But because I grew up with an uncle who could read hands with uncanny brilliance, and because I always had opportunities of meeting others like him, my interest in hands, the stars and the occult generally became, over the years, more than superficial, and I now believe that our patterns of behaviour—and even destinies—are influenced by something the great majority, including myself, will never fully fathom.

What is clear, from observation if nothing else, is that all of us fall into groups with different and distinct characteristics, interests, mannerisms, emotions, reactions, personalities and likes and dislikes, and if one analyses these groups one always comes back to the same conclusion. To some extent we are all victims of our own particular birth sign and conform, to a lesser or greater degree, to an astrological formula laid down by the stars when we are born. Thus my Virgonian husband's thinking is quite different from mine (I'm a temperamental Piscean), but similar to other Virgonians', while my Leonian son not only behaves like a raging lion but even looks like one! Sparks fly permanently, which distresses my sensitive and peace-loving Libran mother but intrigues a close Scorpionian friend who lives with us.

And so the differences go on, but not entirely in temperament. The taste in food of my loved ones also varies enormously (which makes for interesting mealtimes since everyone wants something other than what I've cooked), and this suddenly gave me the idea that perhaps those born under the remaining birth signs also had different tastes in food. I was so fascinated by this theory that I watched people, asked people and scribbled notes over a period of years, and this book, with its information on the twelve birth signs and appropriate recipes for each, is the result of my labours. Writing it gave me a lot of joy and a lot of satisfaction because it brought me a little closer to my fellow men and seemed to improve my own level of tolerance and understanding. My one wish is that those who read it will feel the same and enjoy not only hearing about themselves but also trying out some of the 'bespoke' recipes which I have included.

The information on precious stones is included by courtesy of Hallwag Ltd, Berne, Switzerland, from *Precious Stones*, Orbis Pictus Series (1963).

Sonia Allison.

London, June 1971.

Aries

Aries

THE RAM — 21st March to 20th April

RULING PLANET — MARS

No coward soul is mine,
No trembler in the world's storm-troubled sphere:
I see Heaven's glories shine,
And faith shines equal, arming me from fear.
Emily Brontë.

Character Study — Arieans are average height or taller and are usually large boned but lean and athletic looking. They have long faces and necks, broad foreheads and narrow, sometimes pointed, chins. The eyes—usually grey, brown or hazel—have a direct and clear quality and the dark to sandy coloured hair is frequently thick, coarse and naturally curly. Those Arieans with dark hair have sallow, almost dark complexions while those with fair hair have fresh and light complexions. Towards middle and old age the complexion of all Arieans tends to become ruddy. The nose is strong and well shaped, the mouth is large with thinnish lips and the front teeth sometimes protrude slightly. Arieans are the courageous ones of this world, with a mammoth amount of energy, vitality and drive. They have pioneering spirits, coupled with enthusiasm and pride, and prefer to lead rather than be led. They are fiercely headstrong and ambitious, placing power above money, and have enough self-confidence to get them through even the most difficult situations and crises. They are impulsive, quick to reach and take decisions (rarely do they vacillate) and blunt and frank in their speech, sometimes upsetting those who are slower in deed and word, who are more sensitive and who do not have a full understanding of the Ariean's temperament. Some tend to be too inflexible, too dogmatic and too obstinate for their own good, not always realizing that others have sound opinions also. Most Arieans are idealistic, forceful, enterprising and loyal, with a love of truth, a thirst for knowledge and a desire to reform traditions that they (and perhaps only they) consider to be out-dated, impractical and unconstitutional.

Arieans have many careers open to them and either take up an occupation where they are in a position to govern and control others—such as teaching, lecturing, management, marketing and general business administration—or where they can work on their own initiative in such professions as surgery, dentistry, pharmacy, engineering, journalism and acting. The outdoor life appeals to all Arieans and many are attracted to architecture and surveying, the services (Army, Navy and Air Force), dog-breeding, real estate, building trades, the police force and jobs in travel where they can become couriers, guides and drivers.

Arieans are physically tough people who, because of their over-active minds, sometimes suffer from headaches, neuralgia, insomnia and other nervous disorders associated with the highly strung. They are known to be accident prone and they should therefore beware of burning and cutting themselves.

As a group, Arieans must accept that they can sometimes be difficult to live with and therefore the choice of a husband or wife is something which needs careful and rational consideration. Though they may fall in love quickly and suddenly they must, at all costs, avoid the temptation of marrying in haste and literally repenting at leisure. It is essential to their happiness that they first weigh up the pros and cons of a possible permanent relationship and choose Libran, Leonian or Sagittarian partners who are more capable than those of other signs of understanding the Arean temperament and character. Marriage should never be considered with Capricornians or Cancerians since there would be constant conflict, arguments and unhappinesss.

Cooking — Arieans enjoy cooking, provided whatever it is they are making can be speedily prepared without having to spend hours in the kitchen. They like down-to-earth, healthy dishes with a savoury bias and if they can be made in conjunction with time-saving convenience foods, so much the better. Since much of their life is taken up with entertaining they have a keen interest in quick and easy recipes for colourful and unusual buffet foods and party savouries.

3

Likes — Arieans like warm and vibrant colours including all shades of red, orange and yellow, and clothes that are casual—as opposed to conservative—well-cut and fashionable. They enjoy impulsive holidays more than planned ones and generally choose mountain or ski resorts in preference to the beach. They thrive on physical activity when holidaying, and lying about on the sand all day holds little appeal. Being gregarious, Arieans are great party-goers and givers and adore conversing with all sorts of people. They have a deep fondness for animals—and horses and dogs in particular—and are attracted by sleek, fast cars (which, because of a natural aptitude for driving and excellent road sense, they handle with remarkable expertise), modern furniture, bright and light *décor*, potted plants which flower, quick service in shops and stores and gifts of car gadgets and accessories, radios, tape recorders, books on travel, animals and adventure, unusual pieces of jewellery and good jazz records. Little Arieans are pleased with jigsaws, motor cars, trains, toy clocks and mechanical dolls and puppets.

Dislikes—Arieans dislike criticism, too much discipline, budgeting their money (they prefer to spend rather than save), having to restrain their own frankness, not getting their own way, pale and insipid colours, old-fashioned ideas, dieting for too long, careless driving by others and being told to slow down.

Birth Stone — The birth stone for Arieans is the diamond, the most valuable gem of all. It is one of the hardest stones known and has, when well cut, a characteristic but unique sparkle and brilliance which are unmistakable. Although diamonds are colourless, some have a definite blue, white or yellow tone depending on their quality and place of origin. Diamonds are mined in South Africa, South America and India and the largest diamond in existence is the world-famous 'Cullinan'.

ARIES RECIPES

SPICED COUNTRY SOUP (Serves 4)

1 can (15 oz.) consommé
(2 cups)
4 celery stalks
2 medium carrots
2 oz. mushrooms
1 tablespoon tomato *purée*

1 tablespoon Worcestershire
sauce
¼ pint water (⅔ cup)
¼ pint single cream (⅔ cup
coffee cream)
croûtons

Pour consommé into a saucepan. Cut celery into 2-inch lengths. Cut carrots into fairly thick slices. Slice mushrooms. Add vegetables to consommé with *purée*, Worcestershire sauce and water. Bring to boil and lower heat. Cover and simmer until vegetables are just tender; 25 to 30 minutes. Pour into soup bowls or cups and spoon cream into each. Hand croûtons separately.

STEAK TARTARE (Serves 4 to 6)

A raw meat dish which is, without doubt, an acquired taste! However, it requires the minimum of preparation and no cooking at all, which should please all Arieans!

1 lb. raw fillet or rump steak,
very finely minced
4 very finely chopped anchovies
1 small onion, very finely
chopped

2 tablespoons finely chopped
capers
salt and pepper to taste
2 tablespoons very finely
chopped parsley
4 egg-yolks

Combine steak with anchovies, onion, capers and salt and pepper to taste. Mound equal amounts on 4 individual plates and hollow out centres so that each mound looks like a nest. Sprinkle each hollow with parsley and fill with an egg-yolk. People then mix their own yolks into the meat. Accompany with Continental style rye bread or pumpernickel.

CHICKEN AND CELERY CASSEROLE (Serves 4)

4 large cooked potatoes
3 cooked carrots
4 heaped tablespoons cooked
peas
4 heaped tablespoons sweet corn
4 portions of roasting chicken

1 can (10½ oz.) condensed
cream of celery soup
3 tablespoons dry white wine
2 tablespoons milk
¼ level teaspoon nutmeg

Cut potatoes and carrots into thin slices and arrange over base of fairly large, greased, heatproof dish which is shallow rather than tall. Sprinkle with peas and sweet corn then arrange chicken portions on top. Beat soup until smooth with all remaining ingredients. Pour over chicken then cover dish with lid or aluminium foil. Cook in centre of moderate oven (350°F. or Gas No. 4) for 1¼ hours or until chicken is tender.

CHICKEN TETRAZZINI (Serves 4)

1 can (10½ oz.) condensed
cream of chicken soup
¼ pint milk (⅔ cup)
8 oz. sliced mushrooms
(2½ cups)
12 oz. cold cooked chicken,
diced
1 tablespoon lemon juice

2 oz. shredded almonds
(approximately ¾ cup)
¼ level teaspoon powdered
nutmeg
6 oz. freshly cooked elbow
macaroni
3 oz. finely grated cheddar
cheese (approximately 1 cup)

Put soup and milk into saucepan. Slowly bring to boil, whisking gently all the time. Add mushrooms with chicken, lemon juice, almonds, nutmeg and macaroni. Stir well to mix. Cover and simmer gently for 20 minutes, stirring occasionally. Turn into buttered heatproof dish and sprinkle top thickly with cheese. Brown under a hot grill.

HAM AND BANANA CASSEROLE (Serves 4)

4 medium-sized bananas
4 slices ham
½ pint (1¼ cups) freshly made
white sauce (use packet sauce
mix if preferred)

1 level teaspoon prepared
mustard
4 oz. grated cheddar cheese
(approximately 1¼ cups)

Peel bananas, then wrap a slice of ham round each. Stand in lightly buttered shallow casserole dish. Coat with white sauce mixed with mustard and three-quarters of the cheese. Sprinkle with rest of cheese and re-heat and lightly brown near top of moderately hot oven (375°F. or Gas No. 5) for about 20 minutes. Serve with a cooked green vegetable or mixed salad.

Note: For party use, the ingredients can be doubled or even trebled.

BEEF CREOLE (Serves 4)

4 slices of rump or sirloin steak (sirloin strip steak)
flour
1 oz. butter ($\frac{1}{8}$ cup)
1 medium chopped onion (approximately $\frac{1}{2}$ cup)

1 medium green pepper, chopped
4 oz. sliced mushrooms ($1\frac{1}{4}$ cups)
1 can ($10\frac{1}{2}$ oz.) condensed tomato soup

Dust steak with flour on both sides. Heat butter in flameproof casserole. Add steaks and brown on both sides. Remove to plate. Add onion, green pepper and mushrooms to casserole. Fry slowly until golden brown. Arrange steaks on top then coat with tomato soup. Cover casserole with lid or aluminium foil and cook in centre of moderate oven (350°F. or Gas No. 4) for $1\frac{1}{4}$ hours. Serve with boiled potatoes—tossed in butter and sprinkled with parsley—and a mixed salad.

SPEEDY BOLOGNESE SAUCE (Serves 4)

1 can (about 1 lb. size) minced steak or beef with gravy
2 tablespoons tomato purée
2 skinned and chopped tomatoes
$\frac{1}{4}$ to $\frac{1}{2}$ level teaspoon minced dried garlic

1 tablespoon dried red and green pepper flakes
4 tablespoons water
2 level teaspoons sugar

Put all ingredients into saucepan and bring to boil, stirring. Cover pan and lower heat. Simmer 15 to 20 minutes. Serve over freshly boiled spaghetti and accompany with grated Parmesan cheese.

7

QUICKIE LAMB CASSEROLE (Serves 4)

4 to 5 cold boiled potatoes
4 thick lamb chops, cut from
chump end
1 can (10½ oz.) condensed
cream of mushroom soup
5 tablespoons milk

½ level teaspoon garlic or onion
salt
½ level teaspoon dried marjoram
1 level teaspoon chopped salted
peanuts

Slice potatoes thinly. Arrange over base of buttered shallow heat-proof dish. Stand lamb chops on top. Put soup into saucepan. Add milk, garlic or onion salt and marjoram. Whisk over low heat until smooth. Pour over lamb and potatoes. Cover dish with lid or aluminium foil and cook in centre of moderate oven (350°F. or Gas No. 4) for ¾ to 1 hour. Uncover and sprinkle with peanuts. Serve straight away.

GRAPEFRUIT AND COTTAGE CHEESE SALAD

(Serves 2 as a main dish)

8 oz. cottage cheese (1 cup)
4 tablespoons coarsely chopped
salted peanuts
1 level tablespoon chopped
chives
2 level teaspoons finely chopped
parsley
1 teaspoon paprika

2 tablespoons grated Parmesan
cheese
2 large cup-shaped lettuce
leaves
1 large grapefruit
2 black grapes or maraschino-
flavoured cherries

Combine cottage cheese with peanuts, chives, parsley, paprika and Parmesan cheese. Stand lettuce leaves on 2 individual plates and fill with cheese mixture. Peel grapefruit and divide flesh into segments by cutting in between membranes. Arrange attractively on top of salads then place a grape or cherry on each.

TONGUE WITH SAUCE ROBERT (Serves 4)

An easy version made with bought tongue.

1 rasher lean bacon	2 parsley sprigs
1 small celery stalk	shake of black pepper
3 large mushrooms	salt to taste
2 large onions	1 tablespoon butter
1 small carrot	4 tablespoons dry white wine
1 tablespoon dripping	2 tablespoons wine vinegar
2 level tablespoons flour	2 level teaspoons French
½ pint beef stock (1¼ cups)	mustard
1 dessertspoon tomato *purée*	pinch of sugar
1 bay leaf	12 oz. sliced bought tongue,
	cooked

To make Sauce Robert, coarsely chop bacon, celery, mushrooms and one of the onions. Slice carrot thickly. Heat dripping in pan. Add prepared vegetables. Cover and fry gently for 10 minutes, shaking pan frequently. Stir in the flour. Cook, stirring, until flour becomes deep gold in colour. Gradually blend in stock then add *purée*, bay leaf, parsley, pepper and salt. Bring to boil, stirring. Lower heat, cover pan and simmer gently 45 minutes. Meanwhile, chop second onion. Heat butter in pan, add onion and fry gently until pale gold. Add wine and vinegar and boil gently until reduced by half. Strain sauce. Add to reduced wine and vinegar mixture with mustard and sugar. Mix thoroughly. Stand tongue on 4 hot plates. Coat with sauce and serve straight away.

Note: Any left-over sauce can be refrigerated, re-heated when wanted and served with any roast meat, poultry or duckling.

SAUSAGE MEAT 'PIE' (Serves 4 to 6)

1 lb. pork sausage meat	½ level teaspoon finely grated
4 oz. liver, very finely chopped	lemon peel
1 small onion, finely chopped	½ level teaspoon dried sage
3 level tablespoons fresh white	1 medium egg, beaten
breadcrumbs	salt and pepper to taste
1 level tablespoon chopped	1 large packet frozen puff
parsley	pastry, thawed

Combine sausage meat with liver, onion, breadcrumbs, parsley, lemon peel, sage and beaten egg. Mix very thoroughly then season to taste with salt and pepper. Roll out pastry into an oblong approximately 10 inches by 12 inches. Cover one half of the pastry with sausage filling to within 1 inch of edges. Moisten edges with water then cover with other half of pastry. Press edges well together to seal and transfer to ungreased baking tray. Bake in centre of hot oven (450°F. or Gas No. 8) for 15 minutes. Reduce temperature to moderately hot (400°F. or Gas No. 6) and bake a further 30 minutes. Cut into slices and serve hot with salad.

BUFFET CHILLI CON CARNE (Serves 12)

2 tablespoons salad oil
2 large chopped onions
  (approximately 2 cups)
2 chopped garlic cloves
2 lb. raw minced beef
1 to 3 tablespoons chilli powder

2 cans (each 10½ oz.) condensed
  tomato soup
¾ pint water (2 cups)
2 cans (each approximately
  1 lb.) red kidney beans
juice of 1 lemon
salt to taste

Heat oil in large saucepan. Add onion and garlic and fry gently until golden. Add meat and fry fairly briskly until well browned, breaking it up with a fork all the time. Stir in chilli powder (the amount used will depend on how hot you like your chilli), the soup, water, beans, lemon juice and salt to taste. Mix thoroughly and bring to boil, stirring. Simmer, uncovered, for 20 to 25 minutes. Serve with freshly boiled long-grain rice.

LUNCHEON MEAT STROGANOFF (Serves 10 to 12)

A short-cut version of a popular classic and useful to have as a stand-by when guests are coming and time is pressing.

4 cans luncheon meat
  (approximately 2 lb.)
2 packets onion soup mix
4 level tablespoons flour
2 pints water (5 cups)
4 tablespoons tomato *purée*

2 teaspoons Worcestershire
  sauce
½ pint soured cream (1¼ cups
  dairy soured cream)
4 tablespoons finely chopped
  parsley

Cut luncheon meat into ½-inch cubes. Put soup mix and flour into large saucepan. Gradually blend in water. Bring slowly to boil, whisking gently all the time. Add tomato *purée*, Worcestershire sauce and meat cubes. Cover and simmer 10 minutes. Stir in soured cream and parsley. Serve straight away with freshly cooked noodles.

PARTY MEAT BALLS (Serves 12)

- 3 thick slices white bread
- 3 lb. raw minced beef
- 3 medium sized finely chopped onions (1½ cups)
- 3 beaten eggs
- 1½ teaspoons salt
- 2 teaspoons Worcestershire sauce
- 1 level teaspoon dried thyme
- 1 can (10½ oz.) condensed tomato soup
- 1 can (10½ oz.) condensed mushroom soup
- 2 soup cans water
- salt and pepper to taste

Soak bread in water to cover. Squeeze dry and put into mixing bowl. Add beef, onions, beaten eggs, salt, Worcestershire sauce and thyme. Mix very thoroughly together with fork or finger tips. Shape meat mixture into 1-inch balls (easy to do if you keep running your hands under cold water). Put both soups, plus water, into large but fairly shallow saucepan. Slowly bring to boil, stirring. Season to taste (if necessary) with salt and pepper then drop in meat balls, a few at a time. Cover pan and simmer gently for 30 minutes. Serve with freshly boiled rice or noodles and an outsize green salad tossed with French dressing.

CUCUMBER JELLY SALADS (Serves 12)

- 2 envelopes gelatine or sufficient to set 2 pints (5 cups) liquid
- 5 tablespoons cold water
- 1½ pints chicken stock (3¾ cups)
- 1 large peeled cucumber
- 1 small onion
- 4 lettuce leaves
- 3 cans (each 7 to 8 oz.) salmon or tuna
- mayonnaise
- paprika
- 12 lemon slices

Shower gelatine into cold water and leave 5 minutes. Pour stock into saucepan. Add gelatine. Stir over low heat until dissolved. Pour into bowl or basin and leave in the cool until just beginning to thicken and set. Meanwhile, grate cucumber fairly coarsely and put into bowl. Grate onion as finely as possible and add. Cover, leave to stand about 15 minutes, then drain off any liquid that has come from the cucumber. When jelly is ready, stir in cucumber and onion. Pour into 12 individual moulds (or teacups) first rinsed with cold water. Refrigerate until cold and set. Before serving, line 12 individual plates with lettuce. Drain salmon or tuna, flake up flesh with 2 forks and combine with sufficient mayonnaise to moisten. Unmould jellies onto centres of plates then arrange 2 piles of fish mixture on either side of each mould. Sprinkle lightly with paprika. Slit each lemon slice once from centre to outside edge, shape into twists and stand one on top of each mould.

APPLE SLICE (Serves 6 to 8)

An easily prepared dessert made with frozen puff pastry.

1 small packet frozen puff pastry, thawed	1 lb. cooking apples
4 level tablespoons apricot jam	2 level tablespoons granulated sugar

Roll out pastry into an oblong measuring 12 inches by 6 inches. Trim edges evenly with sharp knife and transfer oblong of pastry to ungreased baking tray. To make raised borders, cut two ½-inch wide strips from each of the long sides. Brush with water and stand on both long edges of oblong. Press gently to seal. Spread pastry (except borders) with 2 tablespoons jam. Peel and core apples and slice evenly. Arrange one layer over jam then sprinkle with sugar. Cover attractively with rest of apple slices. Bake just above centre of hot oven (450°F. or Gas No. 8) for 15 minutes. Reduce temperature to moderate (350°F. or Gas No. 4) and bake further 15 minutes. Remove from oven. Melt remaining jam and spoon it over apples. Serve hot with whipped cream.

DEVILLED CHEESE STICKS (Serves 8 to 10)

6 oz. plain flour (approximately ¾ cup all-purpose)
good shake of cayenne pepper
½ level teaspoon onion salt

½ to 1 level teaspoon curry powder
6 oz. chilled butter (¾ cup)
6 oz. cottage cheese (¾ cup)

Sift flour, pepper, onion salt and curry powder into bowl. Cut up butter with knife until pieces are the size of large peas. Rub cheese through fine sieve directly into flour and butter mixture. Form into dough (with no additional liquid) by drawing mixture together with finger-tips. Wrap in foil or waxed paper and refrigerate for 1 hour. Unwrap, then roll out thinly on floured surface. Cut into ½-inch wide strips of assorted lengths and arrange on ungreased baking trays. Bake towards top of hot oven (425°F. or Gas No. 7) for 15 minutes or until golden brown and puffy. Cool on a wire rack and store in an air-tight tin when cold.

SAVOURY PÂTÉ BISCUITS (Makes about 30)

8 oz. plain flour (approximately 1 cup all-purpose)
½ level teaspoon salt
pinch of cayenne pepper
4 oz. butter or margarine (½ cup)
1 egg-yolk
3 to 4 dessertspoons cold water
4 oz. liver pâté

1 dessertspoon single cream (coffee cream)
1 dessertspoon brandy
1 small garlic clove, very finely chopped
1 egg-white
1 tablespoon blanched and chopped almonds

Sift flour, salt and pepper into bowl. Rub in butter or margarine finely. Mix to a stiff dough with egg-yolk and water. Knead lightly until smooth. Beat pâté with cream, brandy and garlic until smooth. Cut pastry into 2 equal pieces and roll each out into a rectangle measuring approximately 9 inches by 10 inches. Spread one rectangle with pâté mixture then cover with second piece of pastry. Brush with egg-white then sprinkle with almonds. Cut into approximately 30 fingers measuring about 1 inch by 3 inches and transfer to 1 or 2 baking trays. Bake near top of moderately hot oven (400°F. or Gas No. 6) for 20 minutes, then cool on wire rack.

MINTED CITRUS CRUSH (Serves about 8 to 10)

3 lemons
3 large oranges
8 oz. caster sugar (1 cup)
½ pint hot water (1¼ cups)

2 trays ice cubes
1 pint cold water (2½ cups)
1 dozen fresh mint leaves

Wash lemons and oranges thoroughly. Dry well then cut into thin slices (without peeling), discarding end pieces. Remove pips then cut slices into small pieces. Put into large jug. Dissolve sugar in the hot water. Pour on to fruit then add ice cubes and cold water. Stir until ice cubes have almost melted. Add mint leaves and pour into tumblers.

HOT GRAPEFRUIT AND CIDER PUNCH (Serves 8 to 12)

4 large grapefruit
2 pints (5 cups) sweet cider
(apple cider)
4 level tablespoons granulated
sugar

2 cinnamon sticks
4 cloves
12 maraschino flavour cherries
6 teaspoons maraschino flavour
syrup

Halve 3 grapefruit and squeeze out the juice. Put into saucepan with cider, sugar, cinnamon sticks, cloves, maraschino cherries and syrup. Slowly bring to boil, stirring, and boil gently for 10 minutes. Meanwhile, peel remaining grapefruit and cut flesh into segments between membranes. Add to punch, ladle into handled cups and serve while still hot.

Taurus

Taurus

THE BULL — 21st April to 20th May

RULING PLANET — VENUS

He may live without books—what is knowledge but grieving?
He may live without hope—what is hope but deceiving?
He may live without love—what's affection but pining?
But where is the man that can live without dining?

Owen Meredith

Character Study — Taureans are average height or shorter. They are well-built and sturdy and the women of this sign are often more broad-hipped than they would like to be! In middle age, many Taureans of both sexes put on weight, which gives them the appearance of being thickset and stocky. They have short, strong necks and kind sympathetic faces with rounded, soft and gentle eyes (usually brown), full curving lips, dimpled cheeks and broad foreheads. Their hair—which, like the eyes, tends to be dark—is frequently thick and shiny and their movements are dignified and controlled. All Taureans are charming, very affectionate and sociable, preferring a calm and stable life to one of change and excitability. As a group they are conservative in thinking and behaviour, strong-willed, cautious, shrewd, reliable, steadfast, firm, thrifty and obstinate. They are undeterred by setbacks and will reach their goals through stamina, determination, persistence and inherent strength of purpose. They are energetic, practical, quiet and friendly, but have a certain air of reserve and secrecy which makes them, at times, seem distant and cool towards family and intimate friends. Consideration and kindness are also natural attributes of Taureans and many are sincere philanthropists who want to serve others in an unob-trusive and genuine fashion, expecting nothing in return. Taureans are

16

not quarrelsome—in fact they are apt to pour oil on troubled waters more quickly than anybody else—but when on extremely rare occasions they are roused to anger, one is strongly advised to beware and steer clear! They become so enraged and so unreasonable and so temporarily out of control that the best course of action is to leave them entirely alone (just as one would leave an irate bull) until they have calmed down sufficiently to be both rational and approachable.

Taureans like to do well in their chosen careers and many are highly successful in farming, landscape and market gardening, floristry, real estate, architecture, medicine, high class catering, banking, the stock market and politics. Others take up music, singing, dancing, dress-making and tailoring, millinery and beauty culture.

Love and marriage are important to all Taureans and they are affectionate and considerate partners striving wholeheartedly to make their marriages lasting and happy. They will achieve success if they choose carefully, and their ideal partners are Virgonians or Capricornians. They are not in harmony with Leonians and Aquarians and marriage with people of these groups should therefore be avoided.

Although Taureans sometimes have ear and throat troubles, they are generally robust people with a lot of resilience. What they must guard against is overweight and its attendant problems and therefore they should take care with their diets and not indulge too freely in rich foods.

Cooking — All Taureans have a love of good food and wine and an instinctive ability to cook well and tastefully. They do not, as a rule, have the same interest in *haute cuisine* as Librans, but prefer beautifully cooked and beautifully served traditional dishes of quality, however simple and however basic they may be. Many Taurean women are gifted in the art of home baking and produce delicious cakes, biscuits and sweetmeats for family and friends. Preserving is another interest and the Taurean housewife is very adept at making chutneys and jams from the fruits and vegetables she grows.

Likes — Because of the influence of Venus, their ruling planet, all Taureans have an appreciation of the good and beautiful things of life. They like elegant and gracious *décor* in subdued colours with splashes of red and pink, well-fitted kitchens and bathrooms, good quality furniture and thick luxurious carpets. They like dressing neatly in shades of light and dark blue, pink, red and turquoise. They understand and love children deeply and have a happy knack of making friends with young people of all age groups. Gardening gives Taureans an enormous amount of satisfaction and many are noted for their prize blooms and vegetables. Flat-dwellers without gardens enjoy cultivating indoor plants and herbs and surrounding themselves with cut flowers, twigs gathered from country walks and interesting succulents and cacti. Quiet seaside or lakeside family holidays, in unsophisticated resorts, hold great appeal for Taureans because it gives them the opportunity of relaxing completely with their partner and children. They are fond of large cars, budgeting their money, having practical hobbies, nibbling between meals, a well-managed home, entertaining small groups of friends, and gifts of jewellery, flowers, chocolates, fruit, leather goods and ornaments for the home. Little girl Taureans like brightly dressed dolls, sewing kits, nurses' uniforms and cooking sets. Little boy Taureans like aeroplanes, cars, trains, cowboy outfits and tool sets.

Dislikes — Taureans do not like very large and noisy parties, and crudity in any shape or form. They are irritated by bad grooming, ill-mannered and uncontrollable children and badly cooked food. They do not take kindly to fast talking and persuasive sales staff—they prefer to make their own decisions when buying without the help of outsiders—to members of the family borrowing their car without permission and having to cut down on food or go on a strict diet.

Birth Stones — The birth stones for Taureans are the vibrant green and highly valuable emerald, which belongs to the family of beryls, and the semi-precious turquoise. To the ancient Egyptians, the emerald symbolized hope, love and peace and they believed that it could magically heal eye diseases and bring comfort and solace to all who wore it. Some of the best emeralds come from Colombia and one of the largest known weighs 225 carats.

In olden times the turquoise was more highly esteemed than many of the more precious gems and was considered to be a protective stone, especially beneficial for travellers and lovers. The most valuable turquoises are very pale blue with fine marbling, and to the superstitious the colour of the stone appears to change if danger lurks or if their lover has been unfaithful!

TAURUS RECIPES

CHEESECAKE (Serves 8 to 10)

There must be more recipes for cheesecake than any other cake in existence, and nearly every cook to whom one speaks has his or her own special and well-tried formula for making *the* perfect cheesecake. Therefore I offer my recipe with a measure of humility, knowing full well that there must be many, many others which are better, grander and altogether more superior. All the same, mine is the result of toil, struggle, tears and anguish (because for years my cheesecakes always had a mischievous habit of doing all the wrong things irrespective of recipe, method, oven temperature, patience, love and understanding), and now that I've achieved success I admit, with pride, that although my cheesecake may not be perfect in the eyes of veteran and accomplished cheesecake makers, it is as close to the best as I shall ever get!

Semi-sweet biscuits
1½ lb. curd cheese
finely grated peel and juice
of 1 medium lemon
½ teaspoon vanilla essence
5 oz. caster sugar
(approximately ⅔ cup)

4 level tablespoons cornflour
(corn starch)
3 eggs, separated
¼ pint double cream (⅔ cup
whipping cream)

Brush base and sides of an 8-inch spring form pan (these are now available in Britain and consist of a flat metal base round which the sides are clipped) with butter. Coat thickly with finely crushed biscuits, making sure there are no thin patches on base and sides. Put cheese into large bowl. Add lemon peel and juice, vanilla, sugar, cornflour, egg-yolks and cream. Mix thoroughly, without beating, until mixture is smooth. Beat egg-whites to a stiff snow. Gently fold into cheese mixture with a whisk. Spoon into prepared pan and bake just below centre of cool oven (300°F. or Gas No. 2) for 1 hour. Turn off oven, open oven door and leave cake where it is for another ½ hour. When completely cold, remove sides only and allow the cake to remain on its metal base for serving.

Note: Instead of the spring form pan, a loose-bottomed 8-inch cake tin may be used.

ALMOND POUND LOAF (Family size)

4 oz. butter or margarine (½ cup)

4 oz. cooking fat (½ cup shortening)

8 oz. caster sugar (1 cup)

1 teaspoon vanilla

4 large eggs

8 oz. sifted plain flour (1½ cups)

3 tablespoons shredded almonds

Brush a 2 lb. loaf tin with melted fat (or shortening). Line base and sides with greaseproof paper and brush with more fat. Put butter or margarine and fat (or shortening) into bowl and beat until soft. Gradually add sugar and vanilla. Cream until mixture is very light and fluffy and about double its original volume. Beat in eggs, one at a time, adding a tablespoon of flour with each. Fold rest of flour in gently with a large metal spoon. Transfer to prepared tin. Smooth top with knife then sprinkle with almonds. Bake in centre of moderate oven (325°F. or Gas No. 3) for 2 to 2¼ hours or until wooden cocktail stick, pushed gently into centre of loaf, lifts out clean. Leave in tin 10 minutes then turn out and cool on wire rack.

SCANDINAVIAN CHRISTMAS BREAD

1 level teaspoon honey or syrup

¼ pint (⅔ cup) tepid water

4 level teaspoons dried yeast (dry granular yeast)

1 lb. strong plain flour (approximately 2 cups bread flour)

1 level teaspoon salt

1 level teaspoon powdered cinnamon

½ level teaspoon powdered nutmeg

½ level teaspoon powdered ginger

1 level tablespoon caster sugar

12 oz. seedless raisins (approximately 1¾ cups)

2 oz. blanched and chopped almonds (approximately ⅓ cup)

grated peel and juice of 1 large orange

2 eggs

Melt honey or syrup in water. Sprinkle yeast on top. Leave at kitchen temperature for 15 to 20 minutes or until mixture froths up. Sift flour, salt, cinnamon, nutmeg and ginger into a large bowl. Add sugar, raisins, almonds and grated orange peel and toss ingredients lightly together.

Add yeast liquid, orange juice and beaten eggs and mix to a firm dough. Knead 15 minutes or until dough is smooth and elastic and no longer sticky. Put into a greased plastic bag and leave to rise in a warm place for about 45 minutes or until dough doubles in size. Knead 5 minutes on a floured surface then shape to fit a well-greased 2 lb. loaf tin. Slip inside greased plastic bag and leave in a warm place until dough reaches top of tin. Take out of bag then bake in centre of moderately hot oven (400°F. or Gas No. 6) for 20 minutes. Reduce temperature to 375°F. or Gas No. 5 for a further 30 minutes. Leave in the tin 5 minutes then turn out and cool on a wire rack. Cut into slices when cold and spread with butter.

WALNUT ORANGE TORTE (Serves 8 to 10)

3 oz. plain flour (approximately ⅜ cup of all-purpose flour)
pinch of salt
3 large eggs
3 oz. caster sugar (approximately ⅜ cup)
3 level tablespoons finely ground walnuts

½ pint double cream (1¼ cups whipping cream)
2 tablespoons milk
3 tablespoons sifted icing-sugar (confectioner's sugar)
1 level teaspoon very finely grated orange peel
1 tablespoon shelled walnut halves, chopped

Grease base and sides of a 7-inch round cake tin with melted butter. Line with greaseproof paper. Brush with more melted butter. Sieve flour and salt twice onto a sheet of greaseproof paper. Put eggs and sugar into a large basin standing over a saucepan of hot water. Whisk steadily for about 12 minutes or until mixture is very thick (as thick as softly whipped cream), very pale in colour and at least twice its original volume. Gently stir in walnuts with a large metal spoon. Sprinkle flour on top gradually. Slowly and lightly cut and fold into egg mixture. Transfer to prepared tin and bake in centre of cool oven (325°F. or Gas No. 3) for 45 minutes or until well risen and the surface springs back when gently pressed with the finger. Remove from oven and leave in tin 15 minutes. Turn out onto a tea-towel resting on a wire cooling rack and carefully peel away paper. When cake is completely cold, slice into 3 layers. Beat cream with milk and icing sugar until thick then stir in orange peel. Chill for 15 minutes. Sandwich cake layers together with about two-thirds of the whipped and flavoured cream. Spread remainder over top of Torte and then scatter with chopped walnuts. Serve as an after-dinner sweet, for afternoon tea or with coffee in the evening.

UNCOOKED CHOCOLATE BISCUIT CAKES
(Makes about 8 or 10)

4 oz. plain chocolate
  (approximately 4 squares)
4 oz. butter ($\frac{1}{2}$ cup)
1 level tablespoon caster sugar
1 egg, beaten

1 tablespoon finely chopped
  walnuts or toasted almonds
4 oz. semi-sweet biscuits
4 to 5 *glacé* cherries

Break up chocolate and put into basin standing over saucepan of hot, but not boiling, water. Cut butter into small cubes and add. Leave until both have melted, stirring once or twice. Remove basin from heat and beat in sugar, egg and nuts. Break biscuits into tiny pieces and stir into chocolate mixture. Spoon into 8 or 10 paper cake cases standing in ungreased bun tins (muffin pans). Chill in the refrigerator until firm. Before serving, decorate each with $\frac{1}{2}$ a cherry.

MOCHA PETITS FOURS (Makes about 15)

1 egg-white
  pinch of cream of tartar
3 oz. caster sugar
  (approximately $\frac{3}{8}$ cup)

$\frac{1}{2}$ teaspoon instant coffee
  powder
3 oz. chocolate dots ($\frac{1}{2}$ cup
  semi-sweet chocolate pieces)

Brush a large baking tray with salad oil. Line completely with sheet of greaseproof paper, *but do not grease*. Put egg-white and cream of tartar into dry bowl and whisk to a stiff snow. Add two-thirds of the sugar and continue whisking until meringue is very thick and shiny and stands in high, firm peaks. Fold in remaining sugar with coffee powder. Reserve about 15 chocolate dots (chocolate pieces). Fold remainder into meringue. Drop 15 teaspoons of mixture onto prepared tray and top each with a chocolate dot. Bake in centre of cool oven (325°F. or Gas No. 3) for 20 to 25 minutes or until very pale gold. Leave until just warm then remove from paper. Transfer to a wire cooling rack. Store in an air-tight tin when completely cold.

APPLE AND CRANBERRY ROLL (Serves 6)

A mouth-watering hot dessert, richly studded with fresh cranberries and apples. If preferred, blackberries may be used instead of the cranberries.

8 oz. plain flour (approximately 1 cup all-purpose flour)
3 level teaspoons baking powder
½ level teaspoon salt
3 oz. butter or margarine (⅜ cup)

1 tablespoon sugar
2 level teaspoons finely grated orange or lemon peel
4 to 5 tablespoons cold milk to mix

Filling

2 large cooking apples, peeled and thinly sliced

8 oz. fresh cranberries
4 tablespoons caster sugar

Topping

1 tablespoon milk
1 level tablespoon caster sugar

1 tablespoon butter
3 tablespoons water

Sift flour, baking powder and salt into bowl. Rub in butter or margarine finely. Add sugar and orange or lemon peel and toss ingredients lightly together. Mix to fairly soft dough with milk. Turn out onto lightly floured surface and knead quickly until smooth. Roll into a rectangle measuring 12 inches by 10 inches. Cover to within 1 inch of edges with two-thirds of the cranberries and the apple slices. Sprinkle with sugar, moisten edges of dough with water and roll up like a Swiss roll (jelly roll), starting from one of the longer sides. Press all joins and edges well together to seal, then transfer to a buttered oblong heatproof dish. Brush top with milk, sprinkle with sugar then add flakes of butter. Spoon remaining cranberries into dish then pour in water. Bake in centre of hot oven (425°F. or Gas No. 7) for 15 minutes. Lower heat to 350°F or Gas No. 4 and bake further 30 minutes. Serve hot with whipped cream.

COGNAC TRUFFLES (Makes approximately 30)

4 oz. plain chocolate
(approximately 4 squares)
2 oz. butter (¼ cup)
2 tablespoons cognac
2 eggs, separated
2 oz. ground almonds
(approximately ¼ cup)

8 oz. sifted icing sugar
(just under 2 cups
confectioner's sugar)
coconut, cocoa or chocolate
vermicelli for coating

Break up chocolate. Put into basin standing over saucepan of hot, but not boiling, water. Add butter and leave until both have melted, stirring once or twice. Remove basin from pan of water then beat in cognac and egg-yolks. Gradually stir in almonds and icing sugar. Spread out on a flat plate and refrigerate until mixture is firm enough to handle. Shape into balls with damp hands then coat with lightly beaten egg-white. Toss in either coconut, cocoa or chocolate vermicelli. Store about 1 week in the refrigerator but no longer than 1 or 2 days at room temperature.

WEST COUNTRY CREAM TEA (Serves 4)

Throughout the West of England one is always able to indulge oneself in a delicious, farm-fresh cream tea, consisting of large scones with thick and golden clotted cream and strawberry or blackcurrant jam. What I did not realize until quite recently was that traditionalists insist that the tea must also be drunk with pouring cream and not milk and that the scones must never, ever, be buttered. For those who want to bring the atmosphere of the West Country into their own homes, here is the way.

8 oz. plain flour (approximately
1 cup all-purpose flour)
1 level tablespoon caster sugar
4 level teaspoons baking powder
½ level teaspoon salt
2 oz. butter or margarine

¼ pint milk (⅔ cup)
beaten egg for brushing
¼ pint clotted cream or whipped
double cream (⅔ cup whipping
cream)
jam
single cream for the tea

Sift flour, sugar, baking powder and salt into bowl. Rub in butter or margarine finely. Mix to soft dough with milk. Turn out onto floured surface and knead lightly until smooth. Roll out to about ½ inch in thickness and cut into approximately 8 rounds with a 3-inch biscuit cutter. Transfer to buttered baking tray and brush tops with egg. Bake near top of hot oven (450°F. or Gas No. 8) for 7 to 10 minutes or until well-risen and golden. Cool on a wire rack.

Serve scones whole, so that people are able to split their own and then spread them first with the clotted cream and finally with the jam. Make tea the normal strength, pour out and add sufficient cream to taste.

APPLE AND GREEN TOMATO CHUTNEY

3 lb. cooking apples
2 lb. green tomatoes
1 lb. onions
½ level teaspoon EACH powdered cinnamon, mace, allspice, ginger and cloves
1 teaspoon prepared mustard

1 lb. seedless raisins (approximately 2¾ cup)
1½ lb. granulated sugar (3 cups)
1½ pint malt vinegar (3¾ cups)
1 level teaspoon salt

Peel and core apples. Quarter tomatoes. Peel and halve onions. Mince these three ingredients coarsely then put into large saucepan with the spices, mustard and raisins. Cover and simmer very gently, stirring occasionally, until very soft. Add sugar, vinegar and salt and stir over low heat until sugar dissolves. Cook slowly, uncovered, until chutney thickens and is the consistency of jam. Transfer to warm dry jars and cover when cold.

RED TOMATO AND APRICOT CHUTNEY

5 lb. skinned tomatoes
2 lb. onions
½ teaspoon EACH powdered ginger, allspice and cloves
1 garlic clove, very finely chopped

1 lb. dried apricots
1½ lb. sugar (approximately 3 cups)
2 level teaspoons salt
1 pint malt vinegar (2½ cups)

Chop tomatoes roughly. Peel onions and grate coarsely. Put both into saucepan with spices and garlic. Snip apricots into small pieces with

25

scissors. Add to pan. Simmer gently, covered, until fruit is tender, stirring occasionally and adding a little of the vinegar if the mixture appears to be drying out. Add sugar, salt and vinegar and stir over a low heat until sugar dissolves. Cook slowly, uncovered, until chutney thickens and is the consistency of jam. Transfer to warm dry jars and cover when cold.

TOMATO JAM

1 lb. skinned ripe tomatoes
1 lb. granulated sugar
   (approximately 2 cups)

finely grated peel and juice
of 2 medium lemons
$\frac{1}{2}$ level teaspoon powdered
ginger

Chop tomatoes and put into a large bowl. Sprinkle with sugar and leave, covered, for about 6 hours. Put into saucepan and stir over a low heat until sugar dissolves. Add lemon peel, lemon juice and ginger and simmer gently, stirring occasionally, for between 1 to 1$\frac{1}{2}$ hours or until jam is thick and pulpy. Leave until luke-warm before transferring to clean, dry jars. Cover when cold.

PLUM AND ORANGE CONSERVE

3 lb. plums
$\frac{3}{4}$ pint water (2 cups)
3 lb. granulated sugar
   (approximately 6 cups)

coarsely grated peel of 2
medium oranges

Well wash plums. Put into large saucepan with the water. Bring to boil and lower heat. Cover and simmer for about 15 to 20 minutes or until fruit is soft. Add sugar and continue to cook slowly, stirring continuously, until sugar dissolves. Add orange peel and boil gently for about 20 to 25 minutes or until a little conserve, poured on to a cold saucer, wrinkles when touched after 2 minutes (approximately 220°F. on sugar or candy thermometer). Remove stones with a perforated spoon then leave conserve until luke-warm. Transfer to clean dry jars and cover when completely cold.

GOOSEBERRY AND LEMON JELLY

Excellent with hot or cold roast pork, duckling, goose and lamb, and can also be used in place of jam.

3 lb. gooseberries   2 level teaspoons finely grated
   cold water to cover   lemon peel
   granulated sugar

Put gooseberries into saucepan and cover with water. Bring to boil and lower heat. Cover and simmer gently for about 20 minutes or until fruit is tender, stirring occasionally. Strain through jelly bag into bowl, if necessary leaving juice to drip slowly for several hours. Measure juice. To every pint (2½ cups) allow 1 lb. (2 cups) sugar. Put juice and sugar into a saucepan and heat gently, stirring continuously, until sugar dissolves. Add lemon peel then boil about 15 to 20 minutes or until a little of the syrup, poured on to a cold saucer, wrinkles when touched after 2 minutes (approximately 220°F. on sugar or candy thermometer). Transfer to clean dry jars and either cover while still very hot or leave until completely cold before doing so.

MINTED APPLE JELLY

3 lb. apples   granulated sugar
   cold water   1 bunch fresh mint

Cut unpeeled and uncored apples into thick chunks. Put into saucepan and barely cover with water. Bring to boil and lower heat. Cover and cook gently until fruit is soft. Strain through jelly bag into bowl, allowing juice to drip slowly for several hours. Measure juice. To every pint (2½ cups) allow 1 lb. (2 cups) sugar. Put juice and sugar into saucepan and heat gently, stirring continuously, until sugar dissolves. Boil about 15 to 20 minutes or until a little of the syrup, poured on to a cold saucer, wrinkles when touched after 2 minutes (approximately 220°F. on sugar or candy thermometer). Remove from heat and add bunch of mint leaves. Leave in the jelly until mint flavour is adequate for personal taste. Remove mint and discard. Pour jelly into clean dry jars and cover when completely cold.

ROAST BEEF AU POIVRE (Serves 6)

3 lb. rump or sirloin steak, in
one piece
melted butter

3 to 4 tablespoons black
peppercorns

1 hour before roasting, brush meat all over with melted butter. Crush peppercorns with a rolling pin then press on to meat with palms of hands. Put into roasting tin and brush with more butter. Stand in centre of pre-heated hot oven (450°F. or Gas No. 8). Immediately reduce temperature to moderate (350°F or Gas No. 4). Roast 1 hour 15 minutes for fairly rare beef; up to 2 hours for very well-cooked beef, basting at least twice. Serve with baked jacket potatoes and butter, a selection of green vegetables to taste and gravy.

MARINADED FRIED CHICKEN (Serves 4)

¼ pint dry white wine (⅔ cup)
1 thinly sliced onion
¼ level teaspoon crushed
rosemary
½ level teaspoon salt
⅛ level teaspoon pepper
1 dozen chicken drumsticks

1 oz. butter (⅛ cup)
1 tablespoon olive or salad oil
2 level tablespoons cornflour
(corn starch)
¼ pint chicken stock (⅔ cup)
seasoning to taste

Pour wine into a shallow glass or enamel dish. Add onion, rosemary, salt, pepper and the drumsticks. Baste drumsticks with wine. Cover dish and refrigerate 2 hours, turning chicken at least twice. Heat butter and oil in large skillet or frying pan. Add drumsticks and fry briskly for 5 minutes. Turn over and fry further 5 minutes. Cover and fry gently for 20 to 30 minutes or until tender. Remove to a warm platter and keep hot. Strain wine marinade and reserve. Stir cornflour (corn starch) into pan juices. Cook 2 minutes. Gradually blend in marinade and stock. Cook, stirring, until sauce comes to boil and thickens. Adjust seasoning to taste and pour into gravy boat. Serve with the drumsticks.

GRILLED SOLE WITH TARTARE SAUCE (Serves 4)

4 medium size Dover soles,
skinned on both sides
1 oz. melted butter (⅛ cup)
salt and pepper
¼ pint mayonnaise, home-made
for preference (⅔ cup)

1 level tablespoon finely
chopped capers
1 level tablespoon finely
chopped parsley
1 level tablespoon finely
chopped gherkins

Stand 2 soles in foil-lined grill pan. Brush with melted butter and sprinkle with salt and pepper. Grill 5 to 7 minutes, depending on thickness. Turn over, brush with more butter and sprinkle with salt and pepper. Grill a further 5 to 7 minutes. Transfer to individual warm dinner plates and keep hot. Repeat with remaining 2 soles. Serve with tartare sauce, made by combining mayonnaise with capers, parsley and gherkins.

STEAK, KIDNEY AND MUSHROOM PUDDING WITH WINE (Serves 4)

8 oz. plain flour (approximately
1 cup all-purpose flour)
3 level teaspoons baking powder
½ level teaspoon salt
4 oz. finely grated or shredded
beef suet (approximately
¾ cup)
about ¼ pint cold water to
mix (⅔ cup)

1 lb. stewing steak
6 oz. ox kidney
1 level tablespoon flour,
well-seasoned with salt and
pepper
4 oz. sliced mushrooms
(1¼ cups)
1 large onion, thinly sliced
3 tablespoons dry red wine

Sift flour, baking powder and salt into a bowl. Add suet and toss ingredients lightly together. Mix to a fairly soft dough with water. Knead lightly on a floured surface until smooth. Roll out two-thirds and use to line a well-greased 1½-pint pudding basin. Cut steak and kidney into small cubes and coat with flour. Put into pastry-lined basin alternately with layers of mushrooms and onions. Pour in wine. Moisten edges of lining pastry with water then cover with lid, cut from rest of

29

pastry. Press edges well together to seal then cover pudding with double thickness of greased greaseproof paper or aluminium foil. Steam steadily for 3½ hours. Serve from the basin.

LAMB, LIVER AND APPLE PUDDING WITH CIDER (Serves 4)

Make exactly as above but use 1 lb. fillet of lamb (cut from leg) instead of beef, 4 oz. lamb's liver instead of kidney and 1 large cooking apple, peeled and thinly sliced, instead of mushrooms. Substitute 3 tablespoons cider for the red wine. Steam about ½ an hour less.

Gemini

Gemini

THE TWINS — 21st May to 20th June

RULING PLANET — MERCURY

Crabbed age and youth cannot live together:
Youth is full of pleasance, age is full of care;
Youth like summer morn, age like winter weather,
Youth like summer brave, age like winter bare:
Youth is full of sport, age's breath is short,
Youth is nimble, age is lame;
Youth is hot and bold, age is weak and cold,
*   Youth is wild, and age is tame;*
Age, I do abhor thee, youth, I do adore thee:
*   O! My love, my love is young!*
Age I do defy thee:
O! sweet shepherd, hie thee,
*   For methinks thou stay'st too long.*

Shakespeare, *The Passionate Pilgrim*

Character Study — Geminians are tall and slender and carry themselves well. The arms and fingers are long and slim, the hair is often fair to mid brown, the foreheads are high and the eyes are nearly always alert, large and hazel in colour. The nose is well and finely shaped, the complexion tends to be either pale or florid and the facial expressions are intelligent and bright. All Geminians move with mercurial speed and agility and their quicksilver minds have the ability to absorb information at a much faster rate than most other people. In general, Geminians are bright, clever, flirtatious, witty, gay, sociable and friendly and remain youthful in mind, spirit and deed all their lives. They tend to be materialistic, hovering constantly between belief and scepticism and lack emotional depth and feeling. They have a strong leaning towards intellectual pursuits, are deeply interested in all aspects of education and knowledge and many are brilliant and inspirational with a vast amount of creative energy, resourcefulness and ingenuity.

Their versatility and adaptability make the choice of a career a relatively simple affair and they do very well as politicians, actors, journalists, lawyers, diplomats, teachers, translators, secretaries, travel guides, salesmen, compères, preachers, comics and *raconteurs*.

Geminians are victims of their own birth sign—The Twins—and because of it are frequently pulled in two opposing directions at once. They take up two courses of action or study together, they yearn to be in two different places at the same time, they fall in love with two people simultaneously and some marry twice. The Geminian is always having to choose between one or two, and this makes him indecisive, occasionally unreliable, superficial—or two-faced—restless, irritable and impatient. All this in turn lowers the resistance, and the Geminian is liable to pick up everything that's going, with colds, feverish coughs and chest complications heading the list. Some also suffer from insomnia and nervous tension and appear to be accident prone.

Geminians are temperamentally unsuited to Virgonians and Pisceans and from the marriage standpoint would feel more settled and much happier with Librans and Aquarians.

Cooking — Geminians like the light touch in food. Small appetizing meals and snacks appeal to them more than anything else, and although they enjoy cooking and find it relaxing, they have not the patience to go in for elaborate meal preparation involving hours of work. Informality is the keynote of their eating habits and Geminians are always content with tray snacks and the all-in-one type dishes which can be eaten from their laps while they are watching television, reading by themselves or entertaining friends. As they are such enthusiastic party givers, they are keen collectors of party recipes for savoury canapés, buffet snacks and dips.

Likes — Geminians adore glowing sunshine yellow and blue, bright lighting effects and modern music. Dancing and skiing are two of their favourite pastimes and they are enthusiastic students of foreign languages. They like new ideas in fashion, gay accessories, unusual jewellery in silver, leisurely shopping, anything to do with children, trailing plants and holidaying in exciting and exotic places. Large parties appeal strongly to this outgoing and vital group, and as their conversation is always witty and sparkling (no sign of shyness here) they can usually be relied upon to create a friendly, light-hearted atmosphere and help the party merrily on its way. Geminians like gifts of practically everything but will be particularly pleased with modern paintings, silver ornaments, a subscription to a new magazine, the latest and most popular records and books on travel and adventure. Little Geminians are happier with a collection of small presents— mechanical toys, puppets, puzzles, mobiles, paints, crayons and colouring books—than one big one.

Dislikes — Geminians dislike excess discipline, being punctual, having to make plans in advance, gardening, parting with their old cars, working by themselves and solitude. They are irritated by contemporaries whose thoughts and ideas are outdated, and people who are intolerant of children.

Birth Stone — The birth stone of Geminians is the rare and beautiful Alexandrite, a member of the chrysoberyl family. It is a brilliant, clear and sparkling stone which changes colour according to the light; in bright sunshine it turns deep moss green and under artificial light a rich ruby red. It was first discovered in Russia—supposedly on the day that Czar Alexander II became of age—and was thus named after him. Real and cultured pearls, despite the myths and superstitions surrounding them, are also lucky for Geminians.

GEMINI RECIPES

CRISP DIP (Serves 8)

4 oz. salted peanuts (¾ cup)
1 celery stalk
3 tablespoons mayonnaise
1 tablespoon tomato ketchup
1 tablespoon sweet pickle

2 tablespoons single cream (coffee cream)
2 teaspoons finely chopped parsley

Chop peanuts and celery very finely. Combine with mayonnaise. Stir in all remaining ingredients and mix thoroughly to combine. Transfer to small bowl. Stand on platter and surround with dunks of potato crisps, 2-inch lengths of celery and baby cocktail sausages.

TANGY CREAM CHEESE DIP (Serves about 8 to 10)

8 oz. cream cheese
¼ pint thick mayonnaise or
salad dressing (⅔ cup)
1 teaspoon Worcestershire
sauce
1 tablespoon tomato ketchup

1 small onion, grated
1 small garlic clove, finely
chopped
1 hard-boiled egg, finely
chopped
salt and pepper to taste

Beat cream cheese until smooth, then gradually beat in all remaining ingredients. Mix thoroughly, then turn into serving bowl. Stand on large platter and surround with dunks of small savoury biscuits, 2-inch lengths of celery, small cauliflower florets, slices of unpeeled cucumber and large radishes, halved.

CREAMY PRAWN DIP (Serves 8 to 10)

¼ pint mayonnaise (⅔ cup)
¼ pint soured cream (⅔ cup
dairy soured cream)
½ level teaspoon prepared
mustard

1 tablespoon finely chopped
parsley
2 teaspoons sherry
2 teaspoons lemon juice
8 oz. peeled prawns, finely
chopped

Combine all ingredients well together. Transfer to serving bowl and chill for 2 hours. Before serving, stand on platter and surround with thin slices of cucumber and potato crisps for dunking.

PICKLED COCKTAIL MUSHROOMS (Serves 8 to 10)

4 tablespoons red wine vinegar
(⅓ cup)
4 tablespoons salad oil (⅓ cup)
1 very thinly sliced onion
1 teaspoon salt
1 tablespoon finely chopped or
minced fresh parsley

1 teaspoon prepared mustard
1 tablespoon sugar
pinch of cayenne pepper
½ teaspoon Worcestershire
sauce
12 oz. button mushrooms

Put vinegar and oil into a saucepan. Add all remaining ingredients except mushrooms. Bring to boil. Add rinsed mushrooms. Cover and simmer 7 minutes. Remove from heat. Pour into china, glass or plastic bowl or basin. Cover when cold and refrigerate about 12 hours. Before serving, drain mushrooms and serve with cocktail sticks.

HOT QUICHE TARTS (Makes 18)

8 oz. short-crust pastry (pie pastry)
2 oz. finely grated cheddar cheese (approximately ⅔ cup)
¼ pint single cream (⅔ cup coffee cream)

2 eggs
¼ level teaspoon salt
1 level teaspoon prepared mustard

Roll out pastry fairly thinly and cut into 18 rounds with 3-inch biscuit cutter. Use to line 18 lightly-buttered bun tins (muffin pans). Put equal amounts of cheese into each. Beat cream well with eggs, salt and mustard. Spoon into lined tins over cheese. Bake in centre of moderately hot oven (375°F or Gas No. 5) for 15 to 20 minutes or until tarts are golden brown and puffy. Remove from tins and serve hot as a party savoury.

LIPTAUER SPREAD (Serves 10 to 12)

An Austrian or Hungarian savoury (I am not quite sure which!), often served as an appetizer with rye bread or pumpernickel.

4 oz. softened butter (½ cup)
8 oz. curd cheese (approximately 1 cup)
2 anchovies, very finely chopped
1 tablespoon very finely chopped onion
1 tablespoon very finely chopped capers

½ tablespoon very finely chopped gherkins
1 level teaspoon French mustard
1 level tablespoon paprika
¼ level teaspoon caraway seeds
salt and pepper to taste
snipped chives

Beat butter to a light cream then very gradually beat in curd cheese, a little at a time. Stir in anchovies, onion, capers, gherkins, mustard, paprika and caraway seeds. Season to taste with salt and pepper and heap on to a platter. Sprinkle with chives and serve with slices of rye bread or pumpernickel—and knives for spreading.

'HELP-YOURSELF' LOAF (Serves about 8)

A filled loaf which can be put on the table for guests to help themselves. They just break off slices and have them with hot tomato or mushroom soup.

1 large French loaf	slices of cheese
butter	slices of onion
French mustard	slices of salami

Slit the loaf into ½-inch thick diagonal slices, making sure base remains intact. Spread cut surfaces with butter and mustard then put a thin slice of cheese, slice of onion and slice of salami into each slit. Wrap loaf in foil and heat through in a moderately hot oven (400°F. or Gas No. 6) for 20 minutes. Unwrap and serve hot.

HOT CHEESE AND HAM SNACKS (Serves 12)

Toast 8 large slices of white bread on one side only. Spread untoasted sides thinly with butter and cut each into 3 fingers. Cover with strips of ham cut the same size as the fingers. Spread liberally with mayonnaise then sprinkle with grated cheddar cheese. Brown under a hot grill and serve straight away.

STUFFED PRUNE BITES (Makes 3 dozen)

3 dozen large prunes	3 dozen blanched almonds
½ pint (1¼ cups) sweet cider (apple cider)	18 rashers of long streaky bacon

Put prunes into a bowl. Heat cider until hot but not boiling and pour over prunes. Cover and leave to soak overnight. When ready to use, lift prunes out of bowl and stand on paper towels. Slit each open and remove stones. Put a whole almond into each cavity. Cut bacon rashers in half and wrap round prunes. Secure with cocktail sticks and stand in baking tin. Cook near top of hot oven (425°F or Gas No. 7) for 7 to 10 minutes or until hot and crisp. Arrange on a lettuce-lined platter and serve hot.

Note: To vary, put a small cube of cheddar cheese, instead of an almond, inside each prune.

BENGAL NIBBLES (Serves 4 to 6)

3 large slices bread
1 oz. butter ($\frac{1}{8}$ cup)
4 oz. ham
2 to 3 tablespoons thickly
 whipped cream

chutney
grated Parmesan cheese
cayenne pepper

Remove crusts from bread then cut each slice into 4 squares. Fry in the butter until crisp and golden. Stand on paper towels to drain. Chop ham finely and combine with sufficient cream to moisten. Transfer bread squares to baking tray and cover with equal amounts of ham mixture. Top each with a little chutney and sprinkle heavily with Parmesan cheese and lightly with cayenne pepper. Heat through and lightly brown near top of hot oven (425°F. or Gas No. 7) for about 7 minutes. Serve hot.

SMOKED SALMON AND HORSERADISH CANAPÉS (Serves 8 to 12)

butter
2 dozen small savoury biscuits
2 dozen strips of smoked
 salmon, measuring
 approximately 4 inches by
 $1\frac{1}{2}$ inches

horseradish sauce
3 lemon slices
1 dozen cocktail gherkins

Butter biscuits fairly thickly. Spread each strip of salmon very thinly with horseradish sauce. Roll up. Stand rolls on top of biscuits. Cut each lemon slice into 4 wedges. Use to garnish 1 dozen *canapés*. Garnish remainder with gherkins.

BANG (Serves 8)
A light-hearted drink for winter parties.

1 pint ale ($2\frac{1}{2}$ cups)
1 pint cider ($2\frac{1}{2}$ cups)
treacle

grated nutmeg
powdered ginger
1 wineglass gin or whisky

Bring ale just up to boil. Remove from heat and mix with cider. Add sufficient treacle to sweeten then flavour to taste with nutmeg and ginger. Add gin or whisky and serve warm.

CURRY BOWLS (Serves 8)

These are fun for a party and can be made in individual foil dishes for easy serving.

8 oz. long-grain rice
  (approximately 1 cup)
1 medium finely chopped onion
  (½ cup)
1 medium diced cooking apple
2 oz. butter or margarine
  (¼ cup)
3 level tablespoons flour

1 level tablespoon curry
  powder
¾ pint chicken stock (2 cups)
juice of ½ small lemon
1 level teaspoon sugar
1 level teaspoon salt
8 hard-boiled eggs, freshly
  cooked and still hot

Garnish

soured cream (dairy soured
  cream)

small cocktail gherkins
8 shelled prawns

Cook rice in 1 pint (2½ cups) boiling salted water for 15 to 20 minutes or until grains are dry and fluffy and have absorbed all the moisture. Meanwhile, fry onion and apple slowly in the butter or margarine until pale gold. Stir in flour and curry powder, then gradually blend in stock. Cook, stirring all the time, until sauce comes to the boil and thickens. Stir in lemon juice, sugar and salt to taste and leave to simmer, with lid on pan, until rice is ready. Divide rice equally between 8 foil dishes. Add a sliced hard-boiled egg to each then coat with the curry sauce. Top each with a heaped teaspoon of soured cream, 1 gherkin and 1 prawn. Serve straight away.

CRUNCHY TUNA WITH SOURED CREAM SAUCE

(Serves 10 as a party snack)

2 cans (each about 7 oz.)
  tuna
4 large slices white bread
2 oz. butter (¼ cup)
½ pint soured cream (1¼ cups
  dairy soured cream)
2 level teaspoons prepared
  mustard

2 level teaspoons sugar
1 tablespoon lemon juice
1 small onion
2 tablespoons finely chopped
  gherkins
lettuce leaves
paprika

Drain tuna and flake up flesh with 2 forks. Put into bowl. Cut bread into small cubes and fry in the butter until crisp and golden. Add to fish. Beat soured cream with mustard, sugar and lemon juice. Grate onion finely and add to soured cream mixture with gherkins. Combine with fish and bread cubes and toss thoroughly, adding a little salad cream if mixture seems a bit on the dry side. Line 10 small dishes or paper plates with lettuce. Top with equal amounts of fish mixture then sprinkle lightly with paprika.

LIVER AND POTATO LAYER BAKE (Serves 4)

A tasty all-in-one lunch or supper dish.

1 lb. potatoes
1 lb. lamb's or pig's liver
4 rashers chopped streaky
   bacon

1 large chopped onion
   (approximately 1 cup)
salt and pepper
$\frac{1}{4}$ pint stock or water ($\frac{2}{3}$ cup)
   butter or margarine

Peel potatoes and cook in boiling salted water for 10 minutes. Drain and slice thinly. Cut liver into wafer-thin slices. Fill well-buttered heat-proof dish (more shallow than deep) with alternate layers potato slices and liver, sprinkling bacon, onion, salt and pepper between layers and beginning and ending with potato slices. Pour stock or water into dish, cover top with flakes of butter or margarine and bake, uncovered, in centre of a moderately hot oven (375°F. or Gas No. 5) for 45 minutes or until top layer of potato is golden brown.

CELERY AND BACON CHEESE (Serves 4)

I had this for the first time on a blustery March evening while touring South Devon with the family. We put up for a night at a somewhat remote guest house near Dartmouth and this celery cheese was the main dish of our late evening supper. It was warming, tasty and satisfying and so pleased was I with this rather unusual combination that I asked our landlady for the recipe. She was only too happy to oblige and here it is.

1 large head of celery
  boiling salted water
4 rashers streaky bacon
3 level tablespoons flour
½ pint rich milk (1¼ cups)
1 level teaspoon prepared
  mustard

½ teaspoon Worcestershire sauce
8 oz. finely grated cheddar
  cheese (approximately 2½ cups)
  salt and pepper to taste
4 large slices white bread
  bacon dripping for frying

Wash celery stalks and cut into fairly thin slices. Cook in boiling salted water until tender but not too soft; it should be a little on the crisp side. Drain, reserving ¼ pint celery water (⅔ cup). Chop bacon and fry slowly in its own fat until golden. Stir in flour then gradually blend in celery water and milk. Cook, stirring, until sauce comes to boil and thickens. Simmer 3 minutes then stir in mustard, Worcestershire sauce, cheese, salt and pepper to taste, and the celery. Leave over a low heat. Fry bread in the bacon dripping until crisp on both sides. Drain and stand on 4 individual warm plates. Pile high with the celery mixture and serve straight away.

KIDNEYS IN WINE ON TOAST (Serves 4)

8 lamb kidneys
1 level tablespoon flour
1 tablespoon butter
½ garlic clove, very finely
  chopped
1 wineglass red wine

1 wineglass water
1 bay leaf
  pinch of dried thyme
  salt and pepper to taste
4 slices white bread
  butter for spreading toast

Peel, core and slice kidneys. Coat with flour. Heat butter in pan. Add garlic and kidney and fry briskly until both are lightly browned. Stir in wine and water then add bay leaf, thyme and salt and pepper to taste. Slowly bring to boil. Lower heat and cover. Simmer gently for 5 minutes. Meanwhile, toast bread on both sides until golden. Butter lightly then stand on 4 individual plates. Cover each with kidneys and serve straight away.

ISRAELI EGG - PLANT OR AUBERGINE (Serves 4)

3 tablespoons salad oil
2 medium chopped onions
(1 cup)
1 to 3 garlic cloves, finely
chopped

2 medium-sized egg-plants or
aubergines
4 large eggs
salt and pepper to taste
4 slices hot buttered toast

Heat oil in saucepan. Add onions and garlic and fry gently until lightly browned. Meanwhile, peel egg-plants and chop coarsely. Add to pan. Cover and simmer very gently for 30 minutes or until egg-plant is tender. (If mixture tends to stick or dry out, add 1 or 2 tablespoons hot water.) Beat eggs, season well to taste with salt and pepper and stir into egg-plant mixture. Scramble lightly, then pile onto hot buttered toast. Serve straight away.

PIQUANT FRIED SANDWICHES (Serves 4)

8 slices white bread
butter
8 oz. grated cheddar cheese
(approximately 2½ cups)
4 tablespoons salad cream
1 level teaspoon prepared
mustard

1 tablespoon chopped gherkin
or capers
1 tablespoon chopped canned
red pimento
2 medium eggs
2 tablespoons milk
oil or bacon dripping for
frying

Cut crusts off bread then spread slices with butter. Mix together cheese, salad cream, mustard, gherkin or capers and pimento. Spread equal amounts over 4 slices bread then cover with remaining slices, buttered sides down (4 sandwiches). Cut each sandwich into 2 triangles then dip in eggs beaten with the milk. Fry in hot oil or dripping until golden brown on both sides. Drain on paper towels and serve hot with coffee, tea or steaming bowls of soup.

BEER RAREBIT BRUNCH (Serves 4)

4 large slices white or brown
   bread
1 oz. softened butter or
   margarine ($\frac{1}{8}$ cup)
$\frac{1}{2}$ level teaspoon prepared
   mustard
$\frac{1}{2}$ teaspoon Worcestershire
   sauce

$\frac{1}{2}$ teaspoon tomato ketchup
6 oz. grated cheddar cheese
   (approximately 2 cups)
2 tablespoons beer
8 freshly fried bacon rashers
4 freshly fried eggs

Toast bread on one side only. Beat butter or margarine to a cream
with the mustard, Worcestershire sauce and ketchup. Stir in cheese
and beer. Spread equal amounts thickly over untoasted sides of bread
and brown under a hot grill. Top each slice with 2 bacon rashers and an
egg. Serve straight away.

Cancer

Cancer

THE CRAB — 21st June to 21st July

RULING PLANET — THE MOON

We are the music-makers
  And we are the dreamers of dreams,
Wandering by lone sea-breakers,
  And sitting by desolate streams;
World-losers and world-forsakers,
  On whom the pale moon gleams:
Yet we are the movers and shakers
  Of the world for ever, it seems.

Arthur O'Shaughnessy

Character Study — Cancerians are average height with shortish arms and legs, round faces and pale complexions. Women of this sign are curvaceous and gently rounded, while the men are inclined to be stout from a fairly early age. Many Cancerians have short noses, attractively tip-tilted, arched eyebrows, round and rather dreamy eyes in light greys and blue, small mouths and a profusion of soft dark hair.

Cancerians are economical, thrifty but not mean, practical, inventive, ambitious, adaptable, independent, discreet, highly imaginative, intuitional, emotional, romantic, sentimental, versatile, receptive (especially to other people's ideas), affectionate, sociable, tremendously sympathetic and hospitable. They have a strong sense of duty, are loyal and utterly devoted to their families (being good parents comes naturally to Cancerians), are deeply attached to relatives and home life and delight in the company of children, their own and other people's. They are proud of tradition and show a lively and sustained interest in history and anything to do with the past, family heirlooms and antiques. Two of the main characteristics of Cancerians are moodiness and extreme sensitivity and this makes them temperamental, a little over dramatic, enigmatic and shy. They vacillate and waver in their emotions and feelings and are changeable in their friendships and affections. They are often short-tempered, impatient and nervous and can appear to be timid, lacking in drive and too unassuming and cautious for their own good. Yet beneath the cloak of inherent reserve lies a stout heart, and many Cancerians have remarkable tenacity, enterprise, moral courage and insight, enabling them to succeed in life through their own efforts and achieve many of their early ambitions.

Being of a water sign, Cancerians are attracted to the sea and many join the Navy or go into other branches of shipping. The antique business, the tourist industry (especially if travel is involved), interior design, building and decorating, real estate, the wine and spirit trade and nursing and midwifery are also favoured by Cancerians, and because they all have a love of food and cooking many become chefs, home economists, food journalists and authors and executives with food companies.

In marriage they are happiest with their fellow water signs, Scorpionians and Pisceans, but are ill at ease with Arieans and Librans.

Cancerians are not as physically strong as those under some of the other signs and are prone to chest infections, rheumatism and, because of their nervous dispositions, to stomach upsets.

Cooking — Cancerians have an inborn appreciation of good food from the tiny tot stage and consequently both men and women of this sign take pride in cooking skilfully and imaginatively. Being nature lovers, they have a fondness for all kinds of fruit and vegetable salads and their interest in history makes them avid and compulsive collectors of old family recipes: their family's or anybody else's! At the same time, they enjoy experimenting with unusual and exotic dishes from anywhere under the sun, and since entertaining is one of their favourite pastimes, Cancerians are always delighted to find interesting and/or luxurious recipes for their dinner and buffet parties.

Likes — Cancerians like all colours and can wear with success any one that takes their fancy, be it pale and shimmering or bright and vibrant. They adore Christmas and all family celebrations, animals, helping the community by working for a charity, luxurious cars, beautiful homes filled with a combination of antique and modern furniture and paintings, entertaining and being entertained, all old people, a well-stocked garden, shopping and either lazy holidays by sea, river or lake or more energetic holidays in ski and sailing resorts. They respond with child-like glee to presents, and women of this sign are always pleased with perfumes and toiletries, antique jewellery, pure silk scarves, beautifully packaged and luxurious chocolates, daintily embroidered bed linen and bathroom accessories, ultra feminine lingerie and historical novels and travel books. Cancerian men will welcome leather brief cases, good quality handkerchiefs, pure silk ties, toiletries, unusual cuff links and tie pins, seal rings and expensive liqueurs and vintage wines. Little Cancerians will appreciate large boxes of chocolates and candies, pretty dolls (especially those from overseas dressed in national costume), small books and colourful posters, a pet rabbit or guinea pig or cage bird and clothes for themselves.

Dislikes — Delegating any type of job to other people, intolerance shown towards children, old people and animals, team games, driving for too long alone in a car (they prefer a companion to chat to), unfriendly and unco-operative shop assistants and dieting solo.

Birth Stone — The birth stone for Cancerians is a ruby, a valuable and highly priced blood red gem which comes mainly from the Far East and which, like the diamond, has an unmistakable clarity and brilliance. It is said to be the stone of life, of Mother Earth, and is, even today, the most highly esteemed stone in the East.

CANCER RECIPES

APPLE STRUDEL (Serves 8 to 10)

The mystique of Strudel pastry was solved for me one week-end by a talented Continental cook who demonstrated, step by step, exactly what to do to get the pastry just as it should be, a feat not easily achieved by the uninitiated, as I was then. We made two Strudels on Saturday; another two on Sunday. The whole house was filled with the sweet Viennese aroma of apples, cinnamon and almonds and we feasted for two blissful days, like gluttonous lords, on huge portions of warm and spicy Strudel, luxuriously topped with slightly sweetened and softly whipped cream, our version of the famous Austrian and German *Schlagsahne*. Apart from anything else it was enormous fun and I shall always be grateful to my teacher, Ulrike Bielfeldt, for showing me the way.

The secret of good Strudel, apparently, lies in the pastry. It must be as elastic as chewing gum and the only way to achieve this is by *not* using an egg, contradictory to a number of recipes which say that you must. Here, then, is our eggless pastry, which I am delighted to say has never once let me down.

Pastry

8 oz. plain flour (1 cup flour)
pinch of salt

4 dessertspoons salad oil
¼ pint tepid water (⅔ cup)

Filling

2 oz. melted butter (¼ cup)
4 level dessertspoons fresh breadcrumbs
4 level dessertspoons ground almonds
2 lb. very thinly sliced cooking apples
1½ level teaspoons cinnamon

2 oz. raisins or sultanas (½ cup)
6 level dessertspoons caster sugar
4 level dessertspoons flaked almonds, or blanched and chopped almonds

Topping

Icing sugar (confectioner's sugar)

Sift flour and salt into a bowl. Make a well in the centre. Pour in oil and the tepid water. Using fingertips, mix to a soft dough. Knead the dough very thoroughly on a lightly floured board or working surface until it is completely smooth and elastic and no longer sticky. This should take between 10 and 15 minutes. If the dough remains a bit on the wet side, add a little more flour and continue kneading until it no longer sticks to either fingers or board. This part is very important. Put the dough back in the bowl, cover with a cloth and leave it, at kitchen temperature, for half an hour. Cover part of the kitchen table or large working area with a clean patterned tablecloth or pillow case. Flour it well. Stand the dough in the centre. Roll it out as thinly as possible with a floured rolling pin, working from the middle outwards. As soon as you can see the pattern of the tablecloth or pillow case coming through clearly, the middle of the pastry is thin enough. Put the rolling pin down, then gently, with fingertips, pull the edges towards you until they, too, are as thin as the middle part. They will stretch like elastic, but do not pull too vigorously or you will tear the pastry and get holes. The pastry by now will be very large and a peculiar and irregular shape, but don't let that worry you. Brush it all over with melted butter, then sprinkle with breadcrumbs and ground almonds. Cover with apples—to within ½ inch of edges—then sprinkle with cinnamon, raisins or sultanas, sugar and flaked or chopped almonds. Fold edges of pastry over filling (it will look rather like the hem of a dress, although much more uneven!) then roll up the Strudel carefully, Swiss roll (or jelly roll) fashion. Roll it, in turn, from the cloth or pillow case directly onto a buttered baking tray, curving it into a horseshoe if the tray is too small. Press edges well together, then brush Strudel completely with remaining melted butter. Bake near top of a moderately hot oven (375°F. and Gas No. 5) for about 45 minutes or until pale gold. Remove from oven and sift icing or confectioner's sugar thickly over the top. Cut into portions and serve while still warm with whipped cream or ice-cream.

MY OWN MOCK 'STRUDEL' (Serves 8 to 10)

Alas, nameless, but meltingly delicious and very rich and buttery. I sometimes serve it to guests in the evening, with coffee, or as an after-dinner sweet with clotted or thick cream.

Make up 12 oz. rich short-crust pastry (pie pastry) with 12 oz. flour (approximately 1½ cups of all-purpose flour) and 6 oz. mixture of butter and cooking fat (¾ cup butter and shortening). Roll out fairly thinly into a square or rectangle. Now comes the rich part. Spread pastry fairly thickly, to within ¼ inch of edges, with softened butter. Then cover the butter with apricot jam. Sprinkle lightly with cinnamon and scatter flaked and toasted almonds over the top. Moisten edges of pastry with water then roll up like a Swiss roll (jelly roll). Transfer to well-buttered baking tray. Bake just above centre of moderately hot oven (400°F. or Gas No. 6) for about 30 to 40 minutes or until pale gold. Remove from oven and leave to cool slightly. Dust sifted icing sugar (confectioner's sugar) thickly over the top and cut into 8 or 10 wedges. Serve warm.

Note: For convenience, the roll can be made early in the day, left in the refrigerator and baked just before required.

HERRING HORS-D'ŒUVRES (Serves 6)

An unusual mid-European dish which is eaten on Christmas Eve, by itself, as a starter.

2 large salt herrings
1 lb. cold boiled potatoes
1 dozen small gherkins
2 medium cooking apples
1 large onion
2 hard-boiled eggs

3 level teaspoons caster sugar
2 tablespoons wine vinegar
   freshly milled pepper
   lettuce leaves
½ pint natural yogurt (1¼ cups)
4 rashers streaky bacon

Soak herrings overnight in plenty of cold water. Drain thoroughly and chop finely, removing bones and any pieces of skin. Put into mixing bowl. Cut potatoes into small dice. Chop gherkins and peeled apples. Grate onion then coarsely chop eggs. Put prepared vegetables, gherkins, fruit and eggs into bowl with herrings. Add sugar, vinegar and pepper to taste and mix well. Transfer to lettuce-lined serving dish, then coat with the yogurt. Cut bacon into thin strips. Fry until crisp, drain well then sprinkle over salad. Chill at least 1 hour before serving.

PICKLED OYSTERS

This recipe is about one hundred years old and I found it in a handwritten book belonging to some forgotten ancestor. It would make very good buffet party fare.

Take four dozen oysters. Strain the liquor, add six blades of mace, twelve peppercorns, a little grated lemon peel, and two or three bay leaves. Put the liquor to boil; when boiling, add the oysters for two minutes. (Some people put half vinegar, half liquor.) When cold, strain off the liquor. Place the oysters in a small dish and garnish with parsley.

TANGY DRESSED WINTER SALAD (Serves 4)

½ medium lettuce
4 celery stalks
1 large apple
4 oz. grated white cabbage
(approximately 1 cup
shredded)

6 dessertspoons mayonnaise
5 dessertspoons natural yogurt
2 dessertspoons sweet pickle
1 dessertspoon tomato ketchup

Wash lettuce and shake leaves dry. Tear into bite-size pieces and put into salad bowl. Cut celery into diagonal strips. Peel apple and cut into thin slices. Add both to salad bowl. Beat all remaining ingredients well together. Pour over salad and toss well. Serve with beef and pork grills and roasts.

MOONDUST SALAD (Serves 4)

½ large lettuce
French dressing
2 large oranges
4 large pineapple rings (fresh
if possible)
6 dessertspoons soured cream
(dairy soured cream)

3 dessertspoons milk
1 dessertspoon lemon juice
1 teaspoon caster sugar (or
confectioner's sugar)
a shake of onion salt
paprika
2 hard-boiled eggs

Wash lettuce and shake leaves dry. Arrange on platter and sprinkle with dressing. Peel oranges—removing all the pith—and slice thinly. Cut each slice in half. Cut pineapple rings into quarters. Arrange oranges and pineapple on top of lettuce. Beat soured cream with milk, lemon juice, sugar and onion salt. Colour slightly with paprika and spoon over the fruit. Shell eggs and rub through a sieve, in small piles, directly on to salad. Serve with meat or poultry grills and roasts.

LONDON SALAD (Serves 4)

3 medium apples (Cox for
preference)
3 medium onions
3 medium tomatoes

French dressing
2 tablespoons finely chopped
parsley

Peel apples and onions and slice both very thinly. Put into salad bowl. Cut tomatoes into wedges and add to bowl. Toss with sufficient dressing to moisten thoroughly. Sprinkle with chopped parsley and serve straight away with poultry or game dishes.

PIQUANT HOT POTATO SALAD (Serves 4 to 6)

Almost a meal on its own, but goes exceptionally well with Frankfurters, cold roast duck and goose, fried liver and hot roast pork.

6 large cooked potatoes	5 tablespoons milk
6 streaky bacon rashers	2 tablespoons sweet pickle
1 large chopped onion (1 cup)	2 tablespoons wine vinegar
1 can (10½ oz.) condensed	salt and pepper to taste
cream of mushroom soup	2 hard-boiled eggs, sliced
½ teaspoon prepared mustard	2 tablespoons chopped parsley

Dice potatoes. Chop bacon coarsely. Put into frying pan or skillet and fry very gently in its own fat until crisp. Add onion and fry further 5 minutes or until very lightly browned. Stir in soup, mustard, milk, sweet pickle, vinegar and salt and pepper to taste. Heat, stirring, until mixture just comes to boil. Add potato dice and warm through slowly, stirring occasionally. Transfer to a warm dish and cover top with egg slices and parsley. Serve straight away.

SEAFOOD SLAW (Serves 4)

1 small head of white cabbage	1 can (approximately 7 oz.)
½ pint mayonnaise (1¼ cups)	drained and flaked salmon or
3 tablespoons tomato ketchup	tuna
2 teaspoons lemon juice	2 tablespoons peeled prawns
1 teaspoon sugar	2 tablespoons sliced stuffed
1 celery stalk, very finely	olives
chopped	4 large lettuce leaves
	4 lemon wedges

Finely shred or grate cabbage. Put into bowl with all remaining ingredients, except lettuce and lemon. Toss thoroughly. Arrange lettuce on 4 individual plates. Top with equal amounts of Seafood Slaw and garnish each with a wedge of lemon. Serve for a light luncheon with brown bread and butter.

DUCK SALAD CABOUL (Serves 4)

8 to 12 oz. cold cooked duckling
½ pint (1¼ cups) mayonnaise,
  home-made for preference
4 teaspoons curry powder

1 canned or bottled red
  pimento cap
1 red apple
lemon juice
watercress

Slice cold duckling and use to cover a serving platter. Combine mayonnaise with curry powder and spoon over duckling. Cut red pimento into strips and arrange, in trellis design, on top of mayonnaise. Cut apple, without peeling, into thin slices. Dip in lemon juice to prevent browning then arrange at one end of dish. Put sprays of watercress at the other end and serve with a tossed green salad and brown bread and butter.

BAKED PLUM CRISP (Serves 6)

1½ lb. cooking plums
6 oz. granulated sugar
  (approximately ¾ cup)
1 level teaspoon powdered
  cinnamon
4 tablespoons water

4 large slices white bread
3 oz. butter or margarine
  (⅜ cup)
3 tablespoons golden syrup
  (corn syrup)

Halve plums and remove stones. Put into buttered heatproof dish measuring approximately 6 inches by 10 inches and no deeper than 2 inches. Sprinkle with sugar, cinnamon and water. Cut bread into ½-inch cubes. Put butter or margarine and syrup into a saucepan and leave over a low heat until both have melted. Add bread cubes. Toss over and over in saucepan with spoon until each cube is well coated with butter/syrup mixture. Sprinkle over fruit in dish then bake in centre of moderately hot oven (375°F. or Gas No. 5) for 30 to 35 minutes or until bread topping is a warm gold. Serve hot or warm with single cream (coffee cream).

MARINADED FRUIT SALAD (Serves 6 to 8)

A delightful combination which can be served with confidence to anyone who appreciates a mellow and flavourful fruit salad.

1 can (about 1 lb. size)
  pineapple chunks
1 can (about 1 lb. size)
  apricot halves
1 large dessert pear
1 large dessert apple
1 dozen black grapes
1 dozen green grapes

1 level teaspoon finely chopped
  fresh mint
2 tablespoons blanched and
  split almonds
4 tablespoons clover honey
1 to 2 tablespoons Cointreau or
  brandy

Drain pineapple and apricots. Reserve syrup and put fruit into serving dish. Peel and core pear and apple. Cut both into small cubes and add to bowl. Halve grapes and remove pips. Add to bowl with mint and almonds. Heat syrup and honey just long enough for honey to melt. Stir in cointreau or brandy and pour over fruit. Stir well, cover with foil, and refrigerate a minimum of 4 hours, stirring occasionally. Serve with crisp sweet biscuits or wedges of sponge cake.

BERRY AND GRAPEFRUIT ICE (Serves 4 to 5)

Not an ice-cream and not a sorbet. Just a very refreshing frozen sweet which tastes as pretty as it looks.

½ pint sweetened raspberry or
  blackberry *purée* (1¼ cups)
½ pint sweetened grapefruit
  juice (1¼ cups)

2 tablespoons sugar
2 tablespoons hot water
4 to 5 lemon slices

To make raspberry or blackberry *purée*, either rub canned or frozen berries through a sieve or liquidize in a blender. If necessary, sweeten well to taste. Combine with grapefruit juice then add sugar—dissolved in the hot water—and pour into 1 or 2 empty ice-cube trays. Freeze until *just* firm in freezing compartment of refrigerator (in which case it is advisable to lower temperature as when making ice-cream) or leave in deep freeze. Break up with a fork and pile into 4 or 5 glasses. Decorate each with a lemon slice and serve straight away.

RHUBARB AND MANDARIN COMPÔTE (Serves 6)

1 can (11 oz.) mandarin oranges
1 lb. rhubarb
4 oz. granulated sugar
(approximately ½ cup)

½ level teaspoon finely grated
lemon peel
½ level teaspoon powdered
ginger (optional)

Drain mandarins. Pour syrup into saucepan. Trim rhubarb and cut into 1-inch lengths. Add to saucepan with sugar, lemon peel and ginger if used. Bring slowly to boil, stirring. Cover pan and lower heat. Cook very gently for 7 minutes, when rhubarb should be just tender. Remove from heat and stir in mandarins. Pour into bowl, leave to cool, then refrigerate, covered, for a minimum of 4 hours. Transfer equal amounts to sundae glasses and top each with either orange or lemon sorbet.

WASSAIL-BOWL

From the Victorian *Encyclopaedia of Practical Cookery*.

This term originated from the Anglo-Saxon *Wes hál*, signifying literally 'be in health'. Pepys in his gossiping diary alludes to Wassail thus: 'On the 4th of January, 1667, Mrs. Pepys had company to dinner, and at night to sup, and then to cards, and last of all to have a flagon of ale and apples, drunk out of a wood cup, as a Christmas draught, which made all merry.' From the foregoing, it is evident that the Wassail-Bowl of our forefathers consisted essentially of a beverage made of ale, flavoured with spices, sweetened with sugar, and in which there floated about pieces of toast, and thin slices of apple. A very good modern Wassail-Bowl may be made as follows:— Put ½ lb. of loaf sugar in a large bowl, grate a nutmeg over it, and dust over 1 teaspoon of powdered ginger; pour over this 1 pint (2½ cups) of hot beer, ½ pint (1¼ cups) of sherry, and 5 pints (12½ cups) of cold beer; stir this thoroughly, put a cover over the bowl, and let it stand for 2 or 3 hours. Cut 2 or 3 thin slices of bread, toast them brown, cut them into pieces, and put them in the bowl. A pint (2½ cups) of cider may be used instead of the wine; and some roasted apples may also be cut into slices and put in the bowl, or a few slices of lemon.

This amount should be ample for between 12 and 16 people.

STEWED BEEF (A Polish dish)

A surprise packet from Mrs. Beeton's *Book of Household Management*, 1888 edition, for discriminating dinner party guests.

Ingredients—a thick beef or rump steak of about 2 lb.; one onion, some breadcrumbs, pepper and salt, 2 oz. butter.

Mode—Mince the onion fine, mix it with the bread, pepper and salt; make deep incisions in the beef, but do not cut it through; fill the spaces with the bread, etc., roll up the steak and put it in a stewpan with the butter; let it stew very gently for more than two hours; serve it with its own gravy, thickened with a little flour, and flavoured, as may be required, either with tomato sauce, Harvey sauce, or ketchup.

Time—about two hours, or rather more.

Average cost, 2/7d.

Sufficient for six persons.

Seasonable—at any time.

EGG-BAKED AVOCADOS (Serves 4)

One of my own favourites. For all avocado addicts, this is one of the best recipes I know and makes an enjoyable change from avocados packed with the more usual prawns and an indifferent cocktail sauce. The quantity below serves 4; for 8 persons, simply double all the amounts given.

2 medium size celery stalks
4 level tablespoons fresh white breadcrumbs
$\frac{1}{2}$ level teaspoon finely grated lemon peel
$\frac{1}{2}$ to 1 level teaspoon onion salt good shake of pepper
$\frac{1}{4}$ level teaspoon paprika

3 tablespoons single cream (coffee cream)
2 medium sized ripe avocados
2 large hard-boiled eggs, chopped
4 level teaspoons toasted breadcrumbs
4 teaspoons melted butter

Very finely chop celery and combine with crumbs, lemon peel, onion salt, pepper, paprika and cream. Halve avocados and remove stones. Scoop out part of the flesh to make nests for filling. Coarsely chop removed flesh and add to crumb mixture with chopped eggs. Mix well then pile into avocados. Sprinkle with toasted breadcrumbs and butter and bake just above centre of moderately hot oven (375°F. or Gas No. 5) for 15 minutes. Serve straight away.

HONEY-GLAZED CHICKEN (Serves 4 to 6)

1 roasting chicken, weighing about 4 lb.
8 streaky bacon rashers
1 large onion
1 tablespoon butter

6 level tablespoons long-grain rice
½ pint water (1¼ cups)
¼ level teaspoon salt
½ level teaspoon dried rosemary
juice of 1 medium orange
2 tablespoons clear honey

Wash chicken under cold running water and leave to drain. Chop bacon and onion fairly finely. Heat butter in large saucepan. Add bacon and onion and fry gently, with lid on pan, until pale gold and soft; about 10 minutes. Add rice and fry a little more briskly for a further 2 minutes. Pour in water, add salt and rosemary and cook gently, covered, for 15 to 20 minutes or until rice grains have absorbed all the moisture and are plump and fluffy. Leave to cool slightly then spoon into chicken. Stand in roasting tin then put into centre of hot oven (450°F. or Gas No. 8). Immediately reduce temperature to moderate (350°F. or Gas No. 4) and roast 1½ hours. Remove from oven and brush thickly with glaze, made by mixing orange juice and honey well together. Return to oven and roast a further 30 minutes, brushing once more with glaze.

SYRIAN LAMB PATTIES (Serves 4)

1 lb. leg of lamb, cubed
1 medium onion
4 oz. cooked long-grain rice (1 cup)
1 small garlic clove, finely chopped

1 to 2 level teaspoons salt
freshly milled pepper
1 egg, lightly beaten
4 small rings canned pineapple
¼ pint natural yogurt (⅔ cup)

Mince lamb and onion twice and put into bowl. Add rice, garlic, salt, pepper and egg. Mix thoroughly to combine, then shape into 4 large patties. Stand in a lightly greased baking tin. Press a pineapple ring onto each patty, brush with syrup from can of pineapple and bake, uncovered, in centre of moderate oven (350°F. or Gas No. 4) for 35 to 40 minutes. Remove from oven then top each with equal amounts of yogurt. Serve straight away.

Leo

Leo

T H E L I O N — 22nd July to 21st August

RULING PLANET — THE SUN

Born of the sun they travelled a short while towards the sun,
And left the vivid air signed with their honour.

Stephen Spender

Character Study — Leonians are tallish, strongly-built people with large bones, firm muscles and broad shoulders. They carry themselves well and always move with cat-like grace, rather like the lion itself. They have large, beautifully shaped heads, broad foreheads, large flashing eyes—grey, green or hazel—and sensuous, upward curving mouths. In youth, Leonians have honey-coloured skins—which freckle easily— but in later life the complexion may become florid. The hair of this group varies from light to mid brown. It is usually thick, silky and mane-like but in men tends to recede early in life. Nearly all Leonians put on weight in middle age, giving them a thickset, almost heavy appearance. Leonians are not the follow-my-leader type. They are born to govern, to lead rather than to be led, and are ever desirious of being at the head of things and in a position to guide and command others. They are bright, masterful, courageous, passionate and dignified, with an abundance of self-confidence, imagination, will-power and self-control. They are utterly trusting of others (too much so because they get let down and sadly disillusioned), sincere, just, patient, completely frank and open, clear-thinking, warm and generous, ever faithful to family, friends and partners, altruistic, cosmopolitan, very sociable, good-humoured, gregarious, idealistic, practical and independent. Nearly all Leonians respond to flattery—true or false—and are great upholders of tradition, outdated or not. Because they invariably achieve success and wealth, and even honour and distinction, in their own lifetime, some of them, as a result, tend to become boastful, pompous, vain, haughty and arrogant.

Leonians are extraordinarily creative, inventive, constructive and persevering and they are particularly well suited to acting, stage design and management, the arts and entertaining in general, politics, music composition, writing and medicine. Those that take up a business career are attracted to luxury industries, such as food, wine, clothes and accessories, jewellery, cosmetics and fashion design.

Leonians are strong, healthy people who recuperate quickly from almost all illnesses but in later years they are prone to heart conditions and rheumatism centred around the back.

Good-natured and adaptable, this group get on well with most of the other signs but in marriage are most compatible with Arieans and Sagittarians. Cancerians, Pisceans and Scorpionians are likely to be trampled on by Leonians and there could be conflict in long-term relationships with Capricornians and Aquarians.

Cooking — Leonians adore eating and do so with relish, enthusiasm and an almost childlike glee. Many are talented cooks, amateur and professional, and love preparing and eating foods which, like themselves, are colourful, dramatic and exotic, and which appeal strongly to smell, sight and taste. Being hospitable, they entertain frequently and well and make a big feature of robust buffet meals and buffet snacks.

Likes — Leonians love warm glowing colours—orange, red, yellow and purple—*avant-garde* clothes, sunshine holidays in countries where there is a Latin influence, large and exotic flowers, luxurious and big cars and spending money both on themselves and other people. They love to surround themselves with luxury, idolize their own children and prefer to be magnanimous and forgiving rather than hostile; their own flashes of temper are quick to come and quick to go and being on bad terms with anybody for more than a few minutes is something they find difficult to tolerate. They enjoy going to the theatre, opera and ballet and are always pleased to receive gifts of bold jewellery, cosmetics and toiletries, accessories such as ties and scarves, foreign foods and expensive liqueurs. Little Leonians like presents to be on a grand scale; *large* dolls, *large* cars and *large* lavishly illustrated books.

Dislikes — All Leonians hate being alone without anyone to talk to, quiet pedantic people, both very pale and very dark colours, mediocrity in anything, budgeting, dieting and driving at night; their eyesight is more reliable in the daytime and consequently so are their reactions. They are upset by pettiness, too much criticism, unenthusiastic sales staff, bad service in restaurants and hotels, insipid interior *décor* and disloyalty.

Birth Stone — The birth stone for Leonians is the leaf-green peridot, a member of the olivine family. The earliest specimens were found about 1500 B.C. and during the Crusades were brought home by knights and given to the Church as gifts. The richest source of peridots is an island in the Red Sea. Others come from Burma, Australia, Scandinavia and Mexico.

LEO RECIPES

BOUILLABAISSE (Serves 8)

A colourful and multi-flavoured Mediterranean fish soup.

4 tablespoons olive oil (about ¼ cup)
2 medium chopped onions (1 cup)
3 finely chopped garlic cloves
1½ pints fish stock (4 cups)
2 cans whole peeled tomatoes (each about 2 lb. size)
1 level teaspoon finely grated orange peel
1 level teaspoon salt
½ level teaspoon saffron
¼ level teaspoon oregano
pinch of dried tarragon

freshly milled black pepper
2 bay leaves
3 teaspoons sugar
1 lb. cod fillet
1 lb. halibut
½ lb. scallops
2 dozen well-washed and scrubbed mussels
1 lb. fresh, frozen or canned lobster (or other seafood to taste)
8 thick slices French bread
extra olive oil for frying

Heat olive oil in large, heavy-based pan. Add onions and garlic. Fry gently until tender and pale gold. Stir in fish stock, canned tomatoes, orange peel, salt, saffron, oregano, tarragon, pepper to taste, bay leaves and sugar. Slowly bring to boil. Stir and lower heat. Cover pan. Simmer gently 40 minutes. Cut cod and halibut into 1½-inch cubes. Cut each washed scallop into 4. Add all fish to pan of tomato mixture with mussels. Stir well. Simmer 5 minutes. Add chunks of lobster and cook further 5 minutes. Fry bread in oil until crisp. Put into 8 large soup bowls. Fill with piping hot bouillabaisse and serve straight away.

To make fish stock, simmer gently for 30 minutes 2 pints water (5 cups) with 1 lb. fish trimmings, an onion, 3 cloves, 1 bay leaf, 1 carrot and 1 broken celery stalk. Strain.

GAZPACHO (Serves 6)

4 large peeled tomatoes
1 large cucumber, peeled
1 large onion, peeled
1 large green pepper
1¼ pints tomato juice
    (approximately 3 cups)
6 tablespoons olive or salad oil

3 tablespoons wine vinegar
2 tablespoons lemon juice
⅛ teaspoon cayenne pepper
    salt and pepper to taste
1 large garlic clove
2 large slices white bread
2 tablespoons snipped chives

Put 2 tomatoes, half the cucumber, half the onion and half the green pepper (all roughly chopped) into blender with ¼ pint (⅔ cup) tomato juice. Blend until smooth and transfer to large serving bowl. Stir in rest of tomato juice, 4 tablespoons oil, vinegar, lemon juice, cayenne pepper and salt and white pepper to taste. Cover and chill a minimum of 3 hours. Meanwhile, rub inside of small frying pan with cut clove of garlic then pour in remaining oil. Cut bread slices into tiny cubes. Heat oil until hot, add bread cubes and fry until crisp and golden, turning. Drain thoroughly and transfer to bowl. Just before serving, chop remaining tomatoes, cucumber, onion and green pepper separately into tiny pieces. Put each into a bowl by itself. Stir the gazpacho well, sprinkle with chives then serve with bowls of accompaniments.

MENESTRA (Serves 6 to 8)

Spanish, and a very distant relation of the more familiar Minestrone.

2 tablespoons olive oil
1 large chopped onion (about
    1 cup)
8 oz. lean bacon rashers
4 level tablespoons flour
2 pints chicken or beef stock
    (5 cups)
1 red or green pepper

1 lettuce
1 small packet frozen broad
    beans
1 small packet frozen French
    beans
    handful of finely chopped
    parsley
1 bay leaf
    salt and pepper to taste

Heat oil in large saucepan. Add onion and fry gently, with lid on pan, until soft and only just beginning to turn colour. Chop bacon, add to pan and fry a further 5 minutes. Stir in flour then gradually blend in stock. Cook, stirring, until mixture comes to boil. Lower heat and cover pan. Simmer 30 minutes. Meanwhile, halve red or green pepper, remove inside fibres and seeds and cut flesh into thin strips. Wash lettuce, shake dry and shred coarsely. Add pepper strips and shredded lettuce to saucepan with broad beans, French beans, parsley, bay leaf and salt and pepper to taste. Stir well to mix then simmer gently for 30 minutes. Serve piping hot.

CRAB SOUP (Serves 6 to 8)

2 oz. butter ($\frac{1}{4}$ cup)
4 level tablespoons flour
1 pint milk (2$\frac{1}{2}$ cups)
1 pint water (2$\frac{1}{2}$ cups)
  flaked meat from 1 large
  freshly cooked crab
1 level teaspoon prepared
  mustard

$\frac{1}{8}$ teaspoon cayenne pepper
  salt and white pepper to taste
2 oz. grated cheddar cheese
  ($\frac{2}{3}$ cup)
1 wineglass dry sherry
  paprika

Melt butter in large saucepan. Add flour and cook gently for 2 minutes without browning. Gradually blend in milk and water. Cook, whisking all the time, until soup comes to boil and thickens. Simmer 5 minutes. Add crabmeat, mustard, cayenne pepper, salt and pepper to taste, cheese and sherry. Very slowly bring just up to the boil, stirring continuously, and remove at once from heat. Ladle into soup cups or bowls and sprinkle top of each lightly with paprika.

INDIAN STYLE LENTIL DAHL (Serves 4)

1 breakfast cup lentils (1 cup)
  cold water
1 level teaspoon salt
3 medium peeled onions
1 small garlic clove
3 tablespoons salad oil

1 level tablespoon curry powder
2 teaspoons sugar
1 tablespoon cold water
1 dessertspoon desiccated
  coconut
  lemon slices

Soak lentils overnight in cold water. Drain and put into a saucepan with water to cover, the salt and one of the onions, coarsely chopped. Bring to boil, stirring, and simmer gently for 2 hours until lentils are tender, adding a little extra boiling water if mixture seems to be drying out too much. About 15 minutes before serving, chop remaining 2 onions and garlic and fry in the salad oil until pale gold. Stir in the lentils, draining first if any water remains. Mix curry powder and sugar to a smooth paste with the tablespoon of water and add to pan. Stir thoroughly and cook for 2 to 3 minutes. Transfer to a warm dish, sprinkle with coconut and garnish with lemon slices. Serve with curries or with meat grills and roasts and fried eggs.

VEAL AND BEEF PAPRIKA (Serves 4)

This recipe is based on one given to me by an elderly Hungarian lady who always used light and dark meat combined in her paprika dishes instead of one meat alone. She was of the opinion that in this way the flavour was vastly superior, and she was right!

1 lb. stewing beef	2 level tablespoons paprika
1 lb. stewing veal	2 level tablespoons tomato
2 level tablespoons flour	*purée*
1 oz. butter (⅛ cup)	1 tablespoon lemon juice
1 tablespoon salad oil	2 teaspoons sugar
2 large chopped onions	¾ pint chicken stock (2 cups)
(approximately 2 cups)	1 to 2 level teaspoons salt
1 garlic clove, chopped	¼ pint soured cream (⅔ cup
1 medium green pepper, cut	dairy soured cream)
into thin strips	

Cut beef and veal into 1-inch cubes. Coat with flour. Heat butter and oil in a large saucepan. Add onions, garlic and green pepper and fry gently, with lid on pan, until soft and pale gold. Add meat cubes (and any loose flour) and fry fairly briskly until all surfaces are brown and well sealed. Stir in paprika, *purée*, lemon juice and sugar. Gradually blend in stock and salt to taste. Bring to boil, stirring. Lower heat and cover pan. Simmer gently, stirring occasionally, for 2 to 2½ hours or until meats are tender. Stir in cream and re-heat without boiling. Serve with freshly cooked flat ribbon noodles.

BEEF—SAUERBRATEN STYLE (Serves 4)

In true Sauerbraten the meat is marinaded for between one and three days and altogether the preparation is time-consuming and in my opinion not worth the effort. This recipe is much speedier to prepare and at the same time succeeds in retaining the hearty and sweet-sour flavour associated with this 'Old World' favourite.

2 lb. stewing steak	2 tablespoons brown sugar
3 dessertspoons salad oil	1 bay leaf
1 large finely chopped onion	freshly milled black pepper
(approximately 1 cup)	salt to taste
1 level tablespoon flour	2 ginger snaps (crushed)
¾ pint beef stock (2 cups)	1 tablespoon tomato ketchup
2 tablespoons wine vinegar	

Cut steak into 1-inch cubes. Heat oil in large saucepan. Add beef and brown on all sides. Remove to plate. Add onion to oil in pan and fry gently until pale gold. Stir in flour and cook further 2 minutes. Gradually blend in stock followed by vinegar, sugar, bay leaf, 1 or 2 grindings of pepper, salt to taste, ginger snaps and ketchup. Bring to boil, stirring. Replace meat and cover pan. Simmer gently for 2 hours or until meat is cooked. Serve with freshly boiled potatoes or noodles and a cooked green vegetable such as cabbage or sprouts.

LIVER AND KIDNEY BRAISE (Serves 4 to 6)

A robust offal dish which teams well with a large tossed mixed salad and dry red wine.

2 large onions	shake of pepper
2 tablespoons salad oil	½ pint stock or water (1¼ cups)
1 lb. ox liver	2 oz. lean ham, chopped
½ lb. ox kidney	1 lb. peeled potatoes
2 level tablespoons flour	2 slices of lemon
1 level teaspoon salt	

Finely chop or coarsely grate onions. Heat oil in flameproof casserole. Add onion and fry gently, with lid on pan, until soft and pale gold; about 7 minutes. Meanwhile cut liver and kidney into small cubes. Add to casserole and fry a little more briskly until pieces are lightly browned and well sealed. Sprinkle in flour, salt and pepper then gradually blend in stock. Slowly bring to boil, stirring. Add ham. Halve or quarter potatoes—depending on size—and add to casserole. Stand lemon slices on top then cover with lid or aluminium foil. Cook in centre of moderate oven (350°F. or Gas No. 4) for 1 to 1¼ hours.

PORK ROLL (Serves 6 to 8)

1½ lb. pork sausagemeat
6 tablespoons fresh white
breadcrumbs
1 beaten egg
½ teaspoon caraway seeds or
dried sage
1 level teaspoon prepared
mustard
8 oz. sliced mushrooms
(approximately 2½ cups)
2 tablespoons butter
8 rashers streaky bacon

Combine sausagemeat very thoroughly with breadcrumbs, egg, caraway seeds or sage, and mustard. Turn out onto floured surface and press into a rectangle measuring about 10 inches by 7 inches. Fry mushrooms gently in butter for about 5 minutes. Scatter over sausage-meat rectangle. Roll up like a Swiss roll (jelly roll) pinching edges well together to seal. Transfer to ungreased baking tray and drape bacon rashers across top and down sides of roll. Bake in centre of moderate oven (350°F. or Gas No. 4) for 45 to 50 minutes. Serve hot with creamed potatoes and peas.

VEAL EXTRAORDINARY (Serves 4)

In an attempt to convert all those who say they find veal dull and uninteresting, I would ask you try this gin-laced recipe with its sophis-ticated and unusual flavour and exquisite bouquet.

1 oz. butter (⅛ cup)
1 dessertspoon salad oil
1 medium chopped onion
(approximately ½ cup)
1 small chopped garlic clove
(optional)
4 oz. lean chopped ham
1½ lb. stewing veal, cut into
cubes
3 medium peeled tomatoes
2 tablespoons gin
strip of orange peel, 2 inches
long
juice of 1 orange
salt and pepper to taste
¼ pint natural yogurt (⅔ cup)
handful of finely chopped
parsley

Heat butter and oil in saucepan. Add onion, garlic and ham. Cover pan and fry slowly for 10 minutes, shaking pan from time to time. Add veal cubes and fry fairly briskly, turning frequently, until they are well sealed. Chop tomatoes and add to pan with gin, orange peel and orange juice, and pepper and salt to taste. Bring slowly to boil, lower heat and cover pan. Simmer 1 hour or until meat is tender. Just before serving, stir in yogurt and parsley. Re-heat without boiling and adjust seasoning to taste. Accompany with new potatoes tossed in butter and French beans or cauliflower.

Note: If you are wondering why no stock or water has been added, you will find there is adequate moisture coming from the meat, vegetables and gin.

KÖNIGSBERGER KLOPSE (Serves 4)

German-style meat balls which are filling, piquant and unbelievably tasty.

1 large slice fresh white bread, ½-inch thick
warm water
1 lb. lean minced beef
2 medium onions
1 large lemon

4 tablespoons finely chopped parsley
½ level teaspoon salt
1 egg
1 pint beef stock (2½ cups)
2 level tablespoons cornflour (corn starch)
3 level tablespoons capers

Soak bread in warm water. Put beef into bowl. Finely grate onions and peel of the lemon. Add to beef with 2 tablespoons parsley, salt and unbeaten egg. Squeeze bread as dry as possible and add to meat mixture. Mix thoroughly either with fingers or wooden fork. Shape into 12 balls. Pour stock into a large pan. Bring to boil and add meat balls. Lower heat and simmer 20 minutes. Draw pan away from heat, remove meat balls and leave on one side.

Mix cornflour (corn starch) to smooth cream with juice of lemon. Stir in 4 tablespoons hot stock. Pour back into rest of stock. Cook, stirring, until sauce comes to boil and thickens. Add meat balls and capers and cover pan. Re-heat for 10 minutes. Arrange meat balls on warm platter. Coat with sauce then sprinkle with remaining parsley. Serve straight away and accompany with freshly boiled rice, allowing between 2 and 3 oz. raw weight per person.

CHICKEN WITH PRUNES AND CIDER (Serves 4 to 6)

One is always looking for an original way of cooking chicken and this slightly exotic recipe, with its own distinctive flavour, is one way round the problem.

1 roasting chicken weighing about 3 lb.
flour
1 oz. butter (⅛ cup)
2 tablespoons salad oil
4 large celery stalks
1 lb. new carrots
1 garlic clove (optional)

2 medium finely chopped onions (approximately 1 cup)
1 dozen large prunes
1 large sliced lemon
¼ pint dry cider (⅔ cup apple cider)
¼ level teaspoon dried rosemary
½ to 1 level teaspoon salt
white pepper to taste

Coat outside of chicken with flour. Lift bird up and shake off surplus. Heat butter and oil in large flameproof casserole. Add chicken and fry briskly on all sides until crisp and golden. Remove to plate. Chop celery. Peel carrots and leave whole. Peel garlic clove (if used) and chop finely. Add prepared vegetables, with onions and garlic, to casserole. Fry, with lid on pan, until soft and pale gold, allowing between 10 and 15 minutes. Add all remaining ingredients then replace chicken, breast uppermost. Cover with lid and cook gently for 1 hour. Uncover and put into centre of hot oven (425°F. or Gas No. 5) for 15 to 20 minutes to brown chicken.

LEMON CREAM WHIP (Serves 6)

Finely grated peel and juice of 2 small lemons
3 oz. sifted icing sugar (approximately ¾ cup confectioner's sugar)

1 wineglass sweet sherry
½ wineglass brandy
¾ pint double cream (approximately 2 cups whipping cream)

Combine lemon juice with icing sugar, sherry and brandy and stir until smooth. Whip cream until just beginning to thicken. Add lemon juice/alcohol mixture and continue beating until mixture is thick enough to form soft peaks. Spoon into 6 glasses and sprinkle each with lemon peel. Serve straight away with sweet crisp biscuits.

CIDER APPLE FRITTERS (Serves 4)

4 level tablespoons flour
1 level teaspoon caster sugar
4 tablespoons lukewarm cider
  (apple cider)
2 teaspoons salad oil

1 egg-white
  deep oil for frying
2 large cooking apples
  sifted icing sugar
  (confectioner's sugar)

To make batter, sieve flour into bowl. Add sugar, then mix to a thick and smooth batter with cider and salad oil. Beat egg-white to a stiff snow and gently fold into batter mixture. Put oil on to heat slowly. Peel apples and remove cores with apple-corer or potato-peeler. Cut apples into rings and coat with batter. Transfer, a few at a time, to the hot oil and fry until crisp and golden. Drain on paper towels, sprinkle thickly with icing sugar or confectioner's sugar, and serve hot.

SPICED PEAR FRITTERS (Serves 4)

Equally delicious but a tiny bit more complicated to make are these pear fritters, using canned fruit.

Pour syrup from 1 can pear halves (about 1 lb. size) into a saucepan. Add 1 cinnamon stick, 4 cloves, $\frac{1}{2}$ level teaspoon powdered ginger and a 4-inch strip of lemon peel. Bring to boil slowly, cover and simmer 30 minutes. Put pears into a shallow dish and pour over the hot syrup. Cover with lid or foil and refrigerate for about 4 hours. Lift pears out of syrup and drain thoroughly on paper towels. Strain syrup, return to clean saucepan and slowly bring to boil. Make up batter as given in previous recipe, using lukewarm water instead of cider. Coat pear halves with the batter and fry as directed. Drain thoroughly on paper towels then instead of sprinkling fritters with icing sugar or confectioner's sugar, coat each serving with the hot spiced syrup.

BAKED BANANAS IN RUM (Serves 4)

4 large bananas
2 tablespoons orange juice
2 tablespoons dark rum
3 tablespoons brown sugar

1 level teaspoon finely grated
  orange peel
1 dessertspoon butter

Peel bananas and arrange close together in a well-buttered heatproof dish. Moisten with orange juice and rum then sprinkle with sugar and orange peel. Top with flakes of butter then cook in centre of moderately hot oven (350°F. or Gas No. 4) for 20 to 25 minutes. Serve hot with whipped cream or ice-cream.

FRENCH BRANDY 'CAKE' (Serves 12)

A glorious confection for buffets.

1 lb. potatoes
8 oz. plain chocolate (8 squares)
6 oz. softened butter (¾ cup)
6 oz. icing sugar (approximately
  1¼ cups confectioner's sugar)

2 egg-yolks
4 teaspoons brandy
  instant coffee powder

Brush the base and sides of an 8-inch spring form pan with melted butter. Peel potatoes and cut into quarters. Cook in boiling salted water until just tender. Drain and cover with cold water. Break up chocolate and put into basin standing over a saucepan of hot, but not boiling, water. Leave until melted, stirring once or twice. Cream butter with sugar until very light, fluffy and pale in colour. Gradually beat in egg-yolks, brandy and the melted chocolate. Drain potatoes and dry thoroughly in a tea-towel. Rub through a fine sieve directly into the chocolate mixture. Beat thoroughly until well blended. Transfer to prepared pan and smooth top with a knife. Chill at least 6 hours. To serve, dip pan quickly into hot water and unclip sides. Leave 'cake' on the metal base and dust top lightly with instant coffee powder. Cut into 12 wedges and serve with single cream (coffee cream).

BUFFET CHEESE CUP (Serves 10 to 12)

1 whole red-skinned Edam
  cheese
2 level teaspoons prepared
  mustard
1 tablespoon brown ale
1 teaspoon Worcestershire
  sauce

1 level teaspoon dried marjoram
double cream (whipping
  cream)
cream crackers or other
  savoury biscuits to taste

Cut a slice off the top of the Edam then carefully scoop out the cheese, leaving a ¼-inch-thick red skin shell. Grate cheese finely then mix with mustard, ale, Worcestershire sauce and marjoram, adding sufficient double cream to hold mixture together. If necessary, cut a thin slice off the base of the Edam shell to make it stand upright, then fill with cheese mixture. Stand on a platter and surround with crackers or other savoury biscuits. Make sure one or two knives are available so that guests may do their own spreading.

HOT BRANDIED COFFEE NOG (Serves 4 to 6)

3 eggs, separated
3 level tablespoons caster sugar
½ pint very hot strong coffee (1¼ cups)
½ pint hot milk (1¼ cups)
2 tablespoons brandy
powdered cinnamon

Beat egg-yolks and sugar together until very thick and pale in colour. Wash beaters, then whip egg-whites until stiff and peaky. Whisk hot coffee, milk and brandy into egg-yolk mixture then lightly fold in beaten whites. Pour into 4 or 6 cups, sprinkle tops lightly with cinnamon and serve straight away.

GINGER CRISPS (Makes about 18)

2 oz. cooking fat (¼ cup shortening)
2 tablespoons golden syrup (corn syrup)
4 oz. plain flour (approximately ½ cup all-purpose)
1 level teaspoon baking powder
2 level teaspoons ground ginger
1 level teaspoon ground cinnamon
½ level teaspoon bicarbonate of soda
1 level dessertspoon caster sugar

Put cooking fat (or shortening) and syrup into a small saucepan and stand over a very low heat until both have melted. Remove from heat and cool slightly. Sift flour, baking powder, ginger, cinnamon and bicarbonate of soda into a bowl. Add sugar and toss ingredients lightly together to mix. Combine with melted fat and syrup. Shape mixture into 18 small balls and stand on lightly buttered baking trays, leaving plenty of room between each, because they spread. Press balls down lightly with a knife then bake in centre of moderately hot oven (375°F. or Gas No. 5) for about 15 minutes. Transfer to a wire cooling-rack and store in an air-tight tin when cold.

Virgo

Virgo

THE VIRGIN — 22nd August to 21st September

RULING PLANET — MERCURY

The pursuit of perfection, then, is the pursuit of sweetness and light . . . .
He who works for sweetness and light united, works to make Reason
and the will of God prevail.

Matthew Arnold, *Culture and Anarchy.*

Character Study — Virgonians are average height or taller, well-proportioned, with beautifully shaped hands and feet. Their heads tend to
be large, the foreheads prominent, the faces oval and the eyes—usually
grey, green or hazel and deep set—are both wistful and soft. The nose
is often large by comparison with the other facial features but the mouth
is on the small side, with full, generous lips. They have sallow or dark
complexions, thick brown hair and fairly high-pitched voices. Although
in youth Virgonians are graceful and slender, they are inclined to put on
weight later in life. People of this sign are fortunate in that they always
manage to retain their youthful looks and therefore appear to be much
younger than they actually are. Virgonians are, by nature, well-balanced,
down-to-earth people who get on with the job in hand in a completely
matter-of-fact and practical way. They are dignified, cautious, cool-
headed, self-possessed, discriminating and modest and are not given
to bursts of emotion or temper. They apply method, precision and
sense to all they do and, because they rarely seek acclaim on their own
account, prefer to go about their business in a quiet unobtrusive way.
All the same they watch for opportunities and make the most of the
good ones that come their way. Many Virgonians are studious, inventive, ingenious, highly intelligent and intellectual with shrewd, analytical
minds, excellent reasoning powers and an ability to absorb an astound-

ing variety of facts and figures. They love knowledge and remain keen students all their lives. Generally, Virgonians are kind, sympathetic, affectionate without being passionate, extremely conscientious and hard working, loyal to family, friends and partners, thrifty, tidy, scrupulously honest and tolerant of old people, children and animals. But they are utter perfectionists and find it hard to accept values or ideals in others which do not reach their own very high moral standards. Thus they can be irritatingly over-critical, sometimes giving the impression of being petty-minded, preoccupied with trivia and difficult to get along with.

A good number of Virgonians are attracted to the professions and many make excellent doctors, analytical chemists, physicists, teachers and professors, detectives and statisticians. Others become extremely able chefs, editors of technical journals, authors, draughtsmen, civil servants, architects, booksellers, sales representatives, farmers, horti-culturists and photographers.

Virgonians rarely marry impulsively but like to have time to think and then assess whether it is true love or infatuation. They expect high standards in all things from their partners and will not tolerate in-fidelity and disloyalty. They are in harmony with Taureans and Capri-cornians although many are also attracted to and marry their complete opposite—the Piscean. They should avoid Geminians, and to a lesser extent Librans and Aquarians, since there might be fundamental differences in attitude and outlook which could make for strife and tension throughout the partnership.

Virgonians are healthy people who seem to have a natural resistance against infectious illnesses. However, they are prone to eczema and disorders of the stomach, bowels and bladder. They also worry in-wardly and this in turn can upset the appetite and cause temporary sleeplessness.

Cooking — Beneath their veneer of coolness and reserve, Virgonians have highly sensitive nervous systems, which, when upset, take their toll on the digestion. Therefore their tastes in food, as one would expect, are extremely conservative (maybe as a means of self-protection) and they much prefer a simple, uncomplicated meal to anything lavish and rich. Because Virgonians are naturally clever with their hands, they are nearly all good cooks—following every recipe to the letter—with a special leaning towards simple basic dishes, vegetarian food, unusual preserves and anything which requires precision and skill such as icing wedding and birthday cakes, and making omelettes and soufflés.

Likes — Virgonians love soft greys, fawns, blues and greens and good quality, fairly conservative clothes. They like formal, neatly laid out gardens, elegant long-lasting flowers, stimulating and intelligent conversation, enterprising and educational holidays, keeping to a budget, simple interior *décor* with functional furniture, collecting useful gadgets of all descriptions, a top quality car, planning trips and driving (they have excellent road sense and rarely have accidents), and gifts of books on almost any subject, record tokens, notepaper and matching envelopes, diaries, address books, wallets, car accessories and subscriptions to technical and intellectual magazines. Little Virgonians like sensible story books and constructional toys of all kinds.

Dislikes — Lack of finesse in anything and anybody, untidiness, unreliability, unpunctuality, debts of any kind, quarrelling, mixing socially with too many strangers, and putting on weight.

Birth Stone — The birth stone for Virgonians is the gentle sapphire, a member of the corundum family. The deep blue gems—the most valuable of all—come from Kashmir and Burma. Less prized but still beautiful are the pale blue sapphires from Ceylon and the almost navy blue ones from Siam. Sapphires are supposed to symbolize purity, peace and loyalty and are often used in the rings of religious dignitaries.

VIRGO RECIPES

FRESH TOMATO AND RICE SOUP (Serves 6)

1 medium carrot	½ level teaspoon dried basil
2 large onions	1 level dessertspoon sugar
2 celery stalks	1 level teaspoon salt
2 lb. skinned tomatoes	freshly milled black pepper
1 tablespoon salad oil	2 level tablespoons cornflour
1½ pints water (approximately 4 cups)	4 tablespoons cold water
	6 tablespoons cooked rice
1 bay leaf	

Peel carrot and onions and slice both thinly. Chop celery and tomatoes. Heat oil in large saucepan. Add carrot, onions and celery and fry gently, with lid on pan, for about 10 minutes or until soft and pale gold. Add tomatoes, water, bay leaf, basil, sugar, salt and pepper to taste. Bring slowly to boil. Lower heat and cover pan. Simmer gently 1½ hours, stirring occasionally. Rub through sieve—or remove bay leaf and liquidize in blender—then return to clean saucepan. Mix cornflour to smooth cream with the water. Add to soup. Bring to boil, stirring continuously, then add rice. Simmer 3 minutes then ladle into 6 warm soup bowls.

GRILLED HERRINGS WITH HORSERADISH BUTTER (Serves 4)

1 oz. softened butter
1 level teaspoon very finely
   grated horseradish
½ teaspoon lemon juice

4 fresh herrings
a little extra melted butter
parsley for garnishing

Whip softened butter to a light cream then beat in horseradish and lemon juice. Put into a tiny basin (or egg-cup) and chill while preparing herrings. Scale and wash herrings and wipe dry with paper towels. Make 3 diagonal slits on both sides of each herring so that heat can penetrate. Put into grill pan and brush with melted butter. Grill 5 minutes. Turn over, brush with more melted butter and grill a further 5 minutes. Transfer to a heated platter and top each with about a teaspoon of horseradish butter. Garnish with parsley.

SAVOURY SOUFFLÉ OMELETTE (Serves 2)

4 large eggs
1 tablespoon milk
½ level teaspoon salt
   a good shake of pepper

about 1 tablespoon unsalted
butter for frying
parsley for garnishing

Separate eggs. Put yolks into one basin and whites into another. Beat yolks with milk and salt and pepper. Whisk egg-whites to a very stiff snow and gently fold egg-yolk mixture into them. Melt butter in a 9- to 10-inch frying pan then rotate pan so that sides are lightly covered with butter. When hot and just beginning to sizzle, spoon in egg mixture. Leave over a low heat for 3 minutes then stand 3 to 4 inches below preheated hot grill. Leave about 3 minutes or until omelette is light and puffy and the top is golden. Cut in half in the pan then transfer to 2 individual warm plates. Garnish with parsley and serve straight away.

CHEESE AND PARSLEY OMELETTE (Serves 1)

2 medium eggs
2 teaspoons water
  salt and pepper to taste
1 level tablespoon grated
  Parmesan cheese

1 level tablespoon very finely
  chopped parsley
butter for frying

Beat eggs lightly with water. Season to taste with salt and pepper then stir in cheese and parsley. Put butter into 6-inch omelette pan. Heat until hot and foamy but do not allow to brown. Pour in egg mixture. After about 10 seconds, move edges of omelette towards centre of pan with knife or spatula, at the same time tilting pan in all directions so that uncooked egg runs back to edges. Cook further ½ to 1 minute, when base should be golden and top still slightly moist. Fold in half or thirds and slide onto warm plate. Serve straight away.

STEAK DIANE (Serves 4)

4 ½-inch sirloin steaks
  (sirloin strip steaks)
  salt
  freshly milled black pepper
1 level teaspoon dry mustard
4 tablespoons unsalted butter

juice of ½ large lemon
2 teaspoons snipped chives or
  parsley
2 teaspoons Worcestershire
  sauce

Beat steaks with meat mallet or rolling pin until they are ⅓ inch in thickness (or ask butcher to do this for you). Sprinkle steaks on both sides with salt, pepper and mustard. Melt butter in large frying pan or skillet. Add steak and cook 2 minutes per side. Remove to warm serving-dish. Add all remaining ingredients to pan or skillet and quickly bring to boil. Pour over steaks and serve straight away. Accompany with whole new potatoes, baby carrots and garden peas, all tossed lightly in butter.

STEAK PIE (Serves 4)

1½ lb. stewing steak
2 level tablespoons flour
½ level teaspoon dry mustard
  salt and pepper
2 medium sliced onions

¼ pint beef stock (⅔ cup)
¼ level teaspoon dried thyme
  (optional)
8 oz. short-crust or puff pastry
  beaten egg for brushing

78

Cut steak into small cubes. Toss in flour seasoned with mustard and salt and pepper. Put, with onions, into 1½-pint pie dish with rim, doming meat up in the centre. Pour in stock then sprinkle lightly with thyme. Roll out short-crust pastry fairly thinly or flaky pastry to ½ inch in thickness. (If either of these are bought ready prepared, follow manufacturer's instructions.) From pastry cut lid 1½ inches larger all the way round than top of pie dish. Moisten rim of dish with water then line with strips cut from pastry trimmings. Moisten strips with more water and cover with lid. Press edges well together to seal then flake up by cutting with the back of a knife. Press edges into flutes. Brush top with egg and make a small hole in the top to allow steam to escape. Put into centre of hot oven (450°F. or Gas No. 8) and bake 15 minutes. Reduce temperature to moderate (350°F. or Gas No. 4) and bake further 2½ hours, covering pie with sheet of damp greaseproof paper after 1 hour to prevent scorching.

MIXED GRILL (Serves 4)

4 lamb cutlets
4 lamb kidneys
  melted butter
4 small pork sausages
2 pieces lamb's liver (each
  about 2 oz.)

4 halved tomatoes
4 rashers bacon
8 mushrooms
  watercress for garnishing

Heat grill. Cut surplus fat off cutlets. Skin kidneys, cut in half and remove cores. Put cutlets and kidneys into grill pan and brush with butter. Grill 3 minutes then turn over. Add sausages and liver. Brush all ingredients with butter and grill 4 minutes. Turn. Add tomato halves, bacon and mushrooms. Brush ingredients with butter and grill 4 minutes. Transfer to heated platter and garnish with watercress. Serve with thin chips and a cooked green vegetable or mixed salad.

GRILLED LAMB CHOPS WITH BERCY BUTTER

¼ small onion
1 tablespoon dry white wine
1 oz. butter
1 level teaspoon very finely
  chopped parsley

2 chump chops or 4 cutlets
  cut from best end neck
a little melted butter

Grate onion very finely. Put into saucepan with wine. Boil gently until only ½ teaspoon remains. Cool completely. Beat butter to a soft cream, then beat in the ½ teaspoon of onion/wine mixture and the parsley. Put onto a small piece of foil and shape, with knife, into short roll 1 inch in diameter. Wrap and refrigerate 1 hour. Stand chops or cutlets in grill pan and brush with melted butter. Grill 2 minutes. Turn over, brush with more butter and grill 2 minutes. Turn over and continue to grill a further 4 to 5 minutes per side for the chops and 2 to 3 minutes per side for the cutlets. Top each chop or cutlet with 1 or 2 slices of chilled Bercy butter and serve straight away with grilled tomatoes.

Note: To cut slices of Bercy butter easily, dip knife in hot water first.

ESCALOPES OF VEAL (Serves 4)

4 escalopes of veal, each about 4 oz.	about 8 tablespoons fine dried breadcrumbs (untoasted)
2 level tablespoons flour, seasoned with salt and pepper	salad oil for frying
2 medium eggs	lemon wedges for garnishing
1 dessertspoon cold water	

Beat escalopes until wafer thin (or ask butcher to do this for you). Snip round edges with scissors to prevent escalopes from curling up during cooking. Coat evenly with flour then lift each one up and shake off surplus. Beat eggs with water. Dip in escalopes, making sure they are covered on both sides. Toss in crumbs then leave for 30 minutes for coating to harden. Heat 2 to 3 inches of oil in a frying pan or skillet until a cube of bread, dropped into it, sinks to the bottom, rises to the top immediately and turns golden within 50 seconds. Fry escalopes 1 or 2 at a time (depending on size of pan) for about 5 minutes. Drain on paper towels, top each with a wedge of lemon and serve straight away.

Note: In a well-cooked escalope, the coating should never adhere to the meat; there should always be a thin gap and it is in order to achieve this that the escalopes are first covered in flour. Do not attempt to crowd the escalopes in the pan. I was taught to cook this dish by an Austrian food expert and she was adamant about the frying, insisting always that the escalopes must be allowed to float in the oil.

LEMON PANCAKES (Serves 4)

4 oz. plain flour (about ½ cup all-purpose flour)
¼ level teaspoon salt
1 egg
½ pint milk (1¼ cups)
1 dessertspoon salad oil

finely grated peel of 1 small lemon
melted cooking fat for frying (melted shortening)
caster sugar

Sift flour and salt into bowl. Mix to thick batter with egg and half the milk. Beat briskly for a good 5 minutes. Add oil and beat for a further 2 minutes. Gently stir in rest of milk and lemon peel. Brush a 9-inch frying pan with melted cooking fat. Stand over medium heat and leave until hot. Pour in 2 or 3 tablespoons batter and quickly move pan in all directions so that base is covered evenly. Fry until golden brown then turn over and fry other side until mottled and golden. Turn out on to tea-towel. Repeat with rest of batter, making total of 8 pancakes. Sprinkle each pancake with lemon juice (using lemon from which skin was grated) and caster sugar. Roll up and serve straight away.

AUSTRIAN PANCAKES (Serves 4)

Make pancakes as above, omitting lemon peel. When cooked, fill with apricot jam and roll up. Put on to a warm serving dish and sprinkle thickly with sifted icing sugar (confectioner's sugar). Re-heat in a moderate oven (350°F. or Gas No. 4) for 15 minutes.

PEACH SOUFFLÉ (Serves 4)

1 oz. butter (⅛ cup)
2 level tablespoons flour
¼ pint milk (⅔ cup)
1 teaspoon vanilla essence

4 tablespoons peach *purée* (made from canned peaches)
3 eggs, separated
1 extra egg-white

Well butter a 2- to 2½-pint soufflé dish. Melt butter in pan. Stir in flour and cook 2 minutes without browning. Gradually blend in milk. Bring to boil, stirring. Cook about 2 minutes, when sauce should be thick enough to leave sides of pan clean. Remove from heat and beat in vanilla, *purée* and egg-yolks. Put egg-whites into clean dry bowl. Beat

81

until stiff and peaky. Gently fold into sauce mixture with whisk or large metal spoon. When smooth and well blended, transfer to soufflé dish. Bake just above centre of moderately hot oven (375°F. or Gas No. 5) for 45 minutes, when soufflé should be well-risen and golden brown. Serve straight away with single cream (coffee cream).

BAKED SYRUP SPONGE PUDDING (Serves 4)

3 tablespoons golden syrup (corn syrup)

6 oz. plain flour (approximately ¾ cup all-purpose flour)

1 level teaspoon baking powder pinch of salt

4 oz. butter or margarine (½ cup)

4 oz. caster sugar (approximately ½ cup)

½ teaspoon vanilla essence

2 eggs

Well butter a 2-pint pie dish and cover base with syrup. Sift together flour, baking powder and salt. Cream butter or margarine with sugar and vanilla until light and fluffy. Beat in whole eggs, one at a time, adding a tablespoon of sifted dry ingredients with each. Using large metal spoon, gently fold in remaining dry ingredients. When evenly combined, transfer to prepared pie dish. Smooth top with knife and bake in centre of moderate oven (350°F. or Gas No. 4) for approximately 1 hour or until wooden cocktail stick, inserted into centre of pudding, comes out clean. Turn out onto warm serving plate and serve hot with single cream (coffee cream) or custard sauce.

SPICY BLACKCURRANT AND COCONUT CRUMBLE

1 lb. blackcurrants

4 oz. granulated sugar (approximately ½ cup)

Topping

6 oz. plain flour (approximately ¾ cup all-purpose)

1 level teaspoon cinnamon

3 oz. butter or margarine (⅜ cup)

2 oz. caster sugar (approximately ¼ cup)

2 level tablespoons desiccated coconut

½ level teaspoon finely grated lemon peel

82

Stem blackcurrants and wash. Put alternate layers of fruit and granulated sugar into 1½- to 2-pint buttered heatproof dish, ending with fruit. Sift flour and cinnamon into bowl. Rub in butter or margarine finely. Add sugar, coconut and lemon peel and toss ingredients lightly to mix. Sprinkle thickly over fruit in dish and bake in centre of moderate oven (350°F. or Gas No. 4) for 45 minutes to 1 hour. Serve hot with single cream (coffee cream) or custard sauce.

CLASSIC CUSTARD SAUCE (Serves 4 to 6)

2 large eggs   ½ pint milk (1¼ cups)
1 level tablespoon caster sugar

Beat eggs with the sugar and about 4 tablespoons milk. Bring rest of milk to boil. Whisk into egg mixture then strain into top of double saucepan or into basin standing over saucepan of gently simmering water. Cook slowly, stirring all the time, until sauce thickens sufficiently to coat the back of the spoon but on *no account* allow it to become so hot that it begins to boil. Pour at once into a cold jug—which prevents further cooking—and serve hot or cold.

SHERRY TRIFLE (Serves 6)

4 trifle sponge cakes
8 macaroons
2 oz. ground almonds (approximately ⅜ cup)
4 to 5 tablespoons sweet sherry raspberry jam
½ pint classic custard sauce (see previous recipe)

¼ pint double cream (⅔ cup whipping cream)
2 tablespoons sifted icing sugar (confectioner's sugar)
1 egg-white
6 *glacé* cherries

Break sponge cakes and macaroons into small pieces and put into serving bowl with almonds. Moisten with sherry. Leave to stand 30 minutes. Top with spoons of jam, spreading it smoothly with a knife, then cover completely with cold custard sauce. Refrigerate for about 2 hours. Just before serving, whip cream and sugar together until thick. Beat egg-white to a stiff snow and gently fold into cream. Pile over trifle then dot with the cherries, first cut into thin slices.

BREAD AND BUTTER RAISIN PUDDING (Serves 4)

6 large slices white bread
butter
3 level tablespoons caster sugar

2 tablespoons seedless raisins
4 medium eggs
1 pint milk (2½ cups)

Remove crusts from bread then spread slices with butter. Cut each slice into 4 squares. Arrange, in layers, in 2-pint buttered heatproof dish sprinkling sugar and raisins between layers. Beat eggs and milk well together. Pour into dish over bread and leave to stand 30 minutes. Bake in centre of cool oven (325°F. or Gas No. 3) for 1 to 1¼ hours or until well puffed and golden. Serve straight away.

CHANTILLY MERINGUE FINGERS (Makes 8 filled fingers)

2 egg-whites
pinch of cream of tartar
5 oz. caster sugar
(approximately ⅝ cup)
1 teaspoon vanilla essence

¼ pint double cream (⅔ cup whipping cream)
1 tablespoon milk
2 tablespoons sifted icing sugar
(confectioner's sugar)

Line greased baking tray with sheet of greaseproof paper but do not grease. Put egg-whites into a clean dry bowl with cream of tartar. Beat until very stiff. Gradually add two-thirds of the sugar and continue beating until meringue is very shiny and stands in high, firm peaks. Fold in rest of sugar with ½ teaspoon vanilla. With large star-shaped tube and icing bag, pipe about 16 fingers on to prepared tray. Bake in centre of very cool oven (225°F. or Gas No. ¼) for between 1 and 1¼ hours. Carefully peel away from paper and leave to cool on wire rack. Beat cream until thick with rest of vanilla, milk and icing (or confectioner's) sugar. Sandwich fingers together, in pairs, with the cream.

CELEBRATION CAKE

A rich fruit cake suitable for birthdays and christenings.

8 oz. plain flour (approximately 1 cup all-purpose flour)
1 level teaspoon powdered cinnamon
½ level teaspoon powdered nutmeg
¼ level teaspoon EACH powdered ginger and cloves
6 oz. butter (¾ cup)
6 oz. soft brown sugar (¾ cup)
1 level tablespoon orange marmalade

½ level teaspoon finely grated orange peel
4 eggs
1½ lb. mixture of currants, sultanas and seedless raisins (approximately 4 cups)
4 oz. chopped *glacé* cherries
4 oz. chopped walnuts
1 tablespoon brown ale or sherry

Almond Paste

8 oz. ground almonds (approximately 1⅜ cup)
8 oz. sifted icing sugar (approximately 2 cups confectioner's sugar)

8 oz. caster sugar (approximately 1 cup)
2 egg-yolks
1 teaspoon lemon juice
1 teaspoon vanilla essence
½ teaspoon almond essence

Royal Icing

3 egg-whites
1½ lb. sifted icing sugar (approximately 6 cups confectioner's sugar)

1 teaspoon vanilla essence
3 drops glycerine

Brush 8-inch round tin or 7-inch square tin with melted cooking fat (shortening). Line base and sides with double thickness of grease-proof paper. Grease paper thoroughly. Sift together flour and spices. Cream butter and sugar until very light and fluffy. Beat in whole eggs, one at a time, adding tablespoon of dry ingredients with each. Beat in marmalade and orange peel then stir in mixed dried fruit, cherries and walnuts. Stir in rest of dried ingredients with the ale or sherry. Transfer to prepared tin and smooth top with knife. Bake in centre of cool oven (300°F. or Gas No. 2) for 3½ to 4 hours or until knitting needle or skewer, inserted into centre of cake, comes out clean. Remove from oven, then leave 30 minutes before turning out of tin onto a wire cooling rack. When cake is completely cold, wrap in foil and leave at least a week before covering with almond paste.

To make almond paste, put almonds and both sugars into bowl. Mix to fairly stiff paste with egg-yolks, lemon juice and essences. Turn out onto surface dusted with sifted icing or confectioner's sugar and knead until smooth. Brush top and sides of cake with melted jam or golden syrup (corn syrup). Roll out half the paste fairly thickly and use to cover top of cake. Roll out rest of almond paste into a strip the same depth as the cake and wrap round sides. Press edges and joins well together then run a rolling pin over the top and a jam jar round the sides; this helps to get a smooth finish. Leave cake uncovered for about 12 hours for almond paste to harden then wrap loosely in foil and leave at least 1 week before covering with Royal Icing.

To make the icing, beat egg-whites until foamy. Gradually beat in icing or confectioner's sugar, vanilla essence and glycerine, adding a little at a time. Continue beating for about 10 minutes, when icing should be very white and smooth, and firm enough to stand in stiff points when beaters are lifted out of bowl. Stand cake on silver board or wooden board covered with aluminium foil. Spread icing smoothly over top and sides, using a broad-bladed knife dipped in hot water. Leave overnight to harden. Transfer rest of icing to basin and cover first with a damp cloth and then with some aluminium foil. Refrigerate overnight.

To decorate cake, beat a little more sifted icing or confectioner's sugar into left-over icing to make it very stiff. Pipe on decorations to taste round sides and edges of cake and on the top. Leave to harden.

Note: If liked, the icing reserved for piping may be coloured pink, blue, green, mauve, orange or yellow with food colouring.

CANDIED LEMON PEEL

6 medium lemons	1 lb. granulated sugar
1 tablespoon salt	(approximately 2 cups)
1¾ pint water (4⅜ cups)	caster sugar

Cut skin into 6 segments from top to bottom of each lemon. Remove skin from fruit carefully, then cut away all the white pith. Put peel segments into bowl. Add salt and $1\frac{1}{2}$ pints water (just under 4 cups) then cover with a plate so that the peel remains under water. Leave overnight. Drain and wash well. Put into saucepan. Cover with cold water and bring to boil. Drain. Repeat a further 3 times to remove any bitterness from the peel. Dry peel with paper towels then cut into narrow strips with kitchen scissors or a sharp knife. Put remaining water and pound of sugar into saucepan. Heat gently until sugar dissolves, stirring, then add peel strips. Simmer gently until peel is almost transparent. Lift out of pan with perforated spoon and put onto paper towels. Drain thoroughly, then toss in caster sugar, making sure peel strips are thickly coated. Stand on a wire rack (such as a grill pan rack) and leave in a warm dry place (a linen cupboard is a good spot) until the peel itself is dry. Store in an air-tight tin.

Libra

Libra

THE SCALES — 22nd September to 22nd October

RULING PLANET—VENUS

I love all beauteous things,
I seek and adore them;
God hath no better praise,
And Man in his hasty days
Is honoured for them.

Robert Bridges

Character Study — Librans tend to be tall, very handsome and slender people, with long slim hands and legs. They usually have symmetrical and classic features, beautiful complexions, fine skins, soft and expressive eyes—in blue or brown—round faces, high cheekbones, thick straight hair which can be either dark or very fair and well-proportioned limbs. All Librans are inclined to put on weight in middle age, due often to over indulgence in rich food. Those born under this sign are naturally refined, sensitive, intuitive, humane, courteous, charming and great admirers of justice. They are artistic, fond of grace and elegance in all things, perceptive, amiable, generous, affectionate, well-balanced and objective. They are lovers of pleasure and beauty and cherish harmony, comfort and peace above all else. They have excellent critical faculties and are capable of taking a completely dispassionate view of life and its problems. On the other hand, Librans can be moody and whimsical, dithery when asked to make snap decisions and variable in their opinions through the influence and persuasions of others around them.

From a career point of view, Librans seem to fare best in the arts; as painters, musicians, designers, actors, writers of poetry, authors, librarians, editors or theatrical managers. Others are attracted to the law while those who prefer business enterprises succeed in the luxury trades—such as perfumery, jewellery, *haute couture*, millinery and antiques.

The health of Librans is usually sound but they occasionally suffer from kidney and bladder troubles and can become depressed if they are inactive or in an unharmonious environment for any length of time.

Companionship and love are very important to all Librans, but they must find sympathetic partners and should therefore avoid Arieans, Cancerians and Capricornians. The most suitable and most complementary marriage partners for Librans are Aquarians and Geminians.

Cooking — Good food, especially of the *haute cuisine* class, is a passion of all Librans. Everything they eat, and indeed serve, must be very well cooked and beautifully presented and they pay as much attention to a tastefully set table, with elegant china, cutlery and glass, as they do to the food itself. Dining out in a luxurious restaurant, where the cooking is known to be first class, appeals greatly to Librans, and even at home they like to ensure that the standard of their own cuisine is as high as it can possibly be. Many Librans have a sweet tooth and love, rather more than they should, rich desserts and petits fours!

Likes — Librans have excellent taste in clothes and like to wear the best that money can buy, preferring a small wardrobe of quality clothes to a large wardrobe of inferior ones. They are comfortable with muted colours, all shades of blue and sometimes violet, well-arranged vases of fresh and sweetly perfumed flowers around the house, antiques and *objets d'art*, brass and copper, good-looking cars, small and somewhat exclusive stores for shopping, early or late holidays in very good hotels situated in quiet resorts, or alternatively touring holidays, entertaining and being entertained, occasionally indulging their children, going to the theatre, concerts, opera and ballet, and presents of jewellery—antique for preference—gift tokens, beautifully illustrated books, lavishly boxed chocolates, toiletries and small expensive ornaments. Little Librans—both boys and girls—like all that is pretty in the way of playthings and will also appreciate musical instruments, colourfully illustrated story books and party clothes.

Dislikes — Librans dislike lack of refinement, vulgarity, bad taste in anything, ostentation, large and impersonal cocktail parties, dieting, uncomfortable homes, strenuous activity, budgeting and people who are badly groomed and carelessly dressed.

Birth Stone — The birth stone for Librans is the multicoloured and mysterious opal, considered by some to be unlucky (based on a primitive, and unfounded, belief that all iridescent stones bring misfortune), but in the East highly prized as the gem of hope. Opals were a favourite of Queen Victoria and she gave them to each of her daughters as wedding gifts. Opals come mainly from Central America, Australia and Eastern Europe.

LIBRA RECIPES

CONSOMMÉ AUX POIS (Serves 6 to 8)

½ breast from cold cooked chicken
4 tablespoons cooked rice
4 tablespoons cooked green peas
1 chopped truffle (optional)
2 pints consommé (5 cups)
grated Parmesan cheese

Cut chicken into thin shreds and put into soup tureen with rice, peas and the truffle (if used). Bring consommé to the boil and add. Stir well to mix. Accompany with a separate bowl of cheese for sprinkling over the top of each serving.

MACARONI À LA REINE (Serves 6 as an *hors-d'œuvre*)

6 oz. elbow macaroni
2 oz. butter (¼ cup)
3 oz. Stilton cheese
¾ pint double cream (2 cups whipping cream)
¼ level teaspoon powdered mace
⅛ teaspoon cayenne pepper
salt to taste
3 tablespoons fresh white breadcrumbs
about 1 extra oz. butter (⅛ cup)

Lightly butter 6 individual heatproof dishes. Cook macaroni in boiling salted water until tender. Drain thoroughly. Put butter into saucepan. Thinly slice cheese and add with cream, mace and cayenne pepper. Cook over a low heat, stirring continuously until smooth, thick and hot. Season to taste with salt. Add macaroni and mix thoroughly. Transfer equal amounts to prepared dishes. Sprinkle with crumbs and top with flakes of butter. Glaze under a hot grill and serve straight away.

FRIED WHITEBAIT (Serves 4 as a starter)

1 lb. whitebait
salt and pepper
flour
deep oil for frying

wedges of lemon
thin slices of brown bread
and butter

Tip whitebait into a colander and wash under cold running water. Drain well then turn out onto a cloth. Dry very thoroughly, then sprinkle with salt and pepper. Put about a small teacup of flour into a paper bag. Add whitebait. Holding bag firmly at the top, shake it briskly up and down so that the fish get completely and evenly coated with flour. Transfer to a chip basket. Heat a pan of oil (corn or groundnut) until a faint haze rises from it or until a cube of bread, dropped into the oil, rises to the top immediately and turns golden in 50 seconds. Plunge in the basket of coated whitebait and fry until the fish are crisp and just beginning to turn colour; they should be pale straw-coloured but not at all brown. Drain on soft paper towels and serve while still very hot. Accompany with lemon and the brown bread and the butter.

FRENCH-STYLE PÂTÉ WITH GRAND MARNIER

(Serves 8 to 12 as a starter)

A connoisseur's pâté with a superb flavour.

8 to 10 rashers streaky bacon
1 lb. pork
8 oz. veal
8 oz. calves' liver
1 large onion, quartered
1 medium garlic clove

1 level teaspoon marjoram
¾ level teaspoon basil
1½ level teaspoons salt
freshly milled black pepper
2 tablespoons Grand Marnier
2 bay leaves

Remove rinds from bacon and discard. Use rashers to line base and sides of a 2 lb. oblong loaf tin. Cut pork, veal and liver into cubes. Mince twice with the onion. Chop garlic very finely and add to meat mixture with marjoram, basil, salt and black pepper to taste and Grand Marnier. Mix very thoroughly then transfer to prepared tin. Smooth with a knife then place the 2 bay leaves on top. Cover the tin with foil and bake in centre of moderate oven (350°F. or Gas

No. 4) for 2 hours. Remove from oven and uncover. Carefully pour off liquid that is in the tin then stand the base of another, slightly smaller tin, on top of the pâté. Weigh it down with a heavy weight or couple of garden stones and refrigerate at least 6 to 8 hours. Turn out and serve cold with hot toast.

AVOCADO SOUP (Serves 6)

An elegant and exquisitely flavoured soup, suitable for any occasion.

1½ oz. butter (approximately
   1½ tablespoons)
3 level tablespoons flour
¾ pint chicken stock (2 cups)

¾ pint milk (2 cups)
1 large ripe avocado
   salt and pepper to taste
   paprika

Melt butter in large saucepan. Stir in flour and cook slowly for 2 minutes without browning. Gradually blend in chicken stock and milk. Slowly bring to the boil, whisking all the time. Cover and simmer 5 minutes. Meanwhile mash avocado flesh finely with a silver or plated fork. Add to saucepan with salt and pepper to taste. Mix thoroughly. Pour into soup tureen or individual soup bowls. Sprinkle paprika over the top for a splash of colour.

CAVIARE-STUFFED EGGS (Serves 8)

8 large eggs
1 tablespoon mayonnaise
2 tablespoons soured cream
   (dairy soured cream)
2 teaspoons lemon juice

2 tablespoons very finely grated
   onion
5 tablespoons caviare (or
   substitute Danish lump fish
   for economy)
   lettuce leaves

Hard-boil eggs and plunge into cold water. Leave 15 minutes then shell and halve lengthwise. Remove yolks to a basin and mash finely. Beat in mayonnaise, soured cream, lemon juice and onion. Stir in the caviare then pile mixture back into egg-white halves. Cover 8 individual plates with lettuce then stand 2 egg halves on each. Chill lightly then serve with brown bread and butter.

CREAMED KIDNEY VOL-AU-VENTS (Serves 4)

An epicurean main course.

8 lamb kidneys
2 oz. butter (¼ cup)
1 medium chopped onion
   (½ cup)
2 oz. sliced mushrooms
   (approximately ⅔ cup)
1 level tablespoon flour
1 level tablespoon tomato *purée*
1 tablespoon Worcestershire
   sauce

¼ pint chicken stock (⅔ cup)
seasoning to taste
4 large baked vol-au-vent
   cases, each about 4 inches in
   diameter
¼ pint soured cream (⅔ cup
   dairy soured cream)
1 heaped tablespoon chopped
   parsley

Skin, halve and core kidneys then cut into quarters. Melt butter in saucepan. Add onion and fry very gently, with lid on pan, for 5 minutes. Add kidney and mushrooms and fry briskly, uncovered, for 3 minutes. Remove from heat. Stir in flour, *purée* and Worcestershire sauce. Gradually blend in stock. Cook, stirring, until mixture comes to boil and thickens. Season to taste, lower heat and cover. Simmer 15 to 20 minutes. Meanwhile, heat vol-au-vent cases in a moderate oven. Just before serving, stir soured cream into kidneys and re-heat without boiling. Stand vol-au-vent cases on warm serving-dish. Fill with kidney mixture and sprinkle thickly with parsley.

ROAST DUCKLING WITH GOOSEBERRIES
(Serves 4)

1 duckling (4 lb.)
   salt
½ medium onion
1 celery stalk
1 medium can (approximately
   10 oz.) gooseberries
2 tablespoons Worcestershire
   sauce

1 tablespoon lemon juice
¼ pint stock made from
   duckling giblets (⅔ cup)
2 level teaspoons cornflour
   (corn starch)
1 tablespoon cold water
   seasoning to taste

Wash and dry duckling and rub salt into skin. Fill body cavity with half the onion and the celery stalk, broken into 3 or 4 pieces. Place on a grid or rack standing in a large roasting tin. Put into centre of moderate oven (350°F. or Gas No. 4) and roast 2 hours. Meanwhile strain gooseberries and pour syrup into saucepan. Add Worcestershire sauce and lemon juice and boil briskly until mixture is reduced by half. Using pastry brush, brush some of the gooseberry glaze twice over duckling while it is roasting.

Transfer duckling to a warm platter and keep hot. Pour off all but 1 dessertspoon fat from roasting tin. Stand tin over a medium heat and pour in stock. Add cornflour (corn starch) mixed to a smooth cream with the cold water. Cook, stirring continuously, until sauce comes to boil and thickens. Add remaining gooseberry glaze and gooseberries. Adjust seasoning to taste. Heat through gently for 5 minutes. Spoon some of the sauce over the duckling. Pour remainder into gravy boat and pass separately.

LOBSTER À LA BORDELAISE (Serves 4 to 6)

1 oz. unsalted butter ($\frac{1}{8}$ cup)
2 level tablespoons flour
$\frac{1}{2}$ pint (1$\frac{1}{4}$ cups) fish stock*
  a pinch of powdered nutmeg
  salt and pepper to taste
1 small finely grated onion
1 small finely grated carrot
1 wineglass dry red wine
1 lb. cooked lobster meat
5 tablespoons double cream (whipping cream)
  shake of cayenne pepper

Melt butter in a saucepan. Stir in flour and cook slowly, stirring all the time, until mixture becomes colour of pale straw. Remove from heat and very gradually blend in fish stock. Cook, whisking gently all the time, until sauce comes to boil and thickens. Add nutmeg and salt and pepper to taste and simmer 10 minutes. Meanwhile put onion, carrot and wine into a separate pan and cook briskly, uncovered, for 5 minutes. Chop up lobster meat, add to wine mixture then combine with sauce. Heat all together for 5 minutes, stirring occasionally. Stir in cream and cayenne pepper to taste. Serve very hot with freshly boiled rice.

* To make a simple fish stock, simmer for 1 hour about 1 lb. fish trimmings, 1 sliced onion, 1 sliced carrot, 1 bay leaf, 2 cloves and 1 teaspoon salt in 1 pint (2$\frac{1}{2}$ cups) water and 1 wineglass white wine. Strain and use as required.

STEWED CHICKEN À LA RÉGENCE (Serves 4 to 6)

1 oz. butter (⅛ cup)
2 teaspoons salad oil
1 roasting chicken weighing
about 4 lb.
1 medium turnip
1 large onion
1 large carrot
1 dozen button mushrooms

2 or 3 sprigs of parsley
1 level teaspoon salt
pepper to taste
¼ pint Madeira (⅔ cup)
¼ pint chicken stock (⅔ cup)
2 level tablespoons cornflour
(corn starch)
3 tablespoons cold water

Heat butter and oil in large stewpan. Add chicken and fry gently until golden brown all over. Thinly slice turnip, onion and carrot. Add to pan with washed mushrooms, parsley, salt, pepper, Madeira and stock. Bring to boil and lower heat. Cover and simmer slowly for about 1 to 1½ hours or until bird is tender. Lift chicken out onto a warm platter and keep hot. Strain pan liquor and pour into clean saucepan. Add cornflour mixed to a smooth cream with the cold water. Slowly bring to boil, stirring. Simmer 1 minute then pour into a gravy boat. Serve with chicken.

POACHED SALMON WITH HOLLANDAISE SAUCE (Serves 4)

1 pint water (2½ cups)
1 wineglass dry white wine
juice of ½ lemon
1 level teaspoon salt
3 peppercorns

1 blade mace
2 sprigs parsley
1 small sliced onion
4 fresh salmon steaks, each
about 1 inch in thickness

Hollandaise Sauce

3 egg-yolks
3 tablespoons boiling water
2 tablespoons lemon juice,
heated to lukewarm

4 oz. unsalted butter (½ cup),
melted and cooled
salt and pepper

Put the water, wine, lemon juice, salt, peppercorns, mace, parsley and onion in a large shallow saucepan or skillet. Bring to boil and lower heat. Cover pan and simmer gently for 30 minutes then add salmon steaks. Reduce heat under pan or skillet so that liquid barely moves. Cover and poach salmon for approximately 20 minutes. Meanwhile make the Hollandaise sauce. Put egg-yolks into a bowl standing over a saucepan of gently simmering water, making sure base of bowl is not in contact with the water. Add a tablespoon of boiling water to yolks and beat until they begin to thicken. Add second tablespoon of water and whisk until yolks thicken even more. Finally beat in last tablespoon of water with luke-warm lemon juice. Still beating all the time, add half the butter, a teaspoon at a time. When the sauce is thick, fluffy and light in colour, add remaining melted butter in a slow continuous trickle, beating without stopping. Season to taste with salt and pepper and transfer to sauceboat. Lift salmon out of pan or skillet with a fish slice and stand on paper towels, for a few minutes, to drain. Transfer to 4 individual warm plates and serve straight away with the sauce. Accompany with new potatoes and peas, both tossed with butter.

TOURNEDOS BÉARNAISE (Serves 4)

Buy 4 tournedos steaks each about $1\frac{1}{2}$ inches thick and 3 inches in diameter. Stand in grill-pan and brush with melted butter. Grill 1 minute. Turn over and brush with more melted butter. Grill a further minute. Turn over and continue to grill a further 3 to 4 minutes per side for underdone/rare steak, a further 5 to 6 minutes per side for medium steak and a further 8 to 9 minutes per side for very well-cooked steak. Remove from grill-pan, stand each tournedos on a round of freshly fried bread and transfer to warm individual plates. Garnish with very fresh and crisp watercress and accompany with Béarnaise sauce.

To make this classic sauce, put 4 tablespoons dry white wine, 2 tablespoons tarragon vinegar, 1 small grated onion and a parsley sprig into a small saucepan. Boil briskly until only 2 tablespoons of liquid remain. Strain. Stir in a dessertspoon of warm water. Make up the Hollandaise sauce as given in the previous recipe, using the strained white wine liquor instead of the lemon juice. After seasoning the sauce with salt and pepper, stir in $\frac{1}{4}$ level teaspoon dried tarragon or 1 to 2 leaves of finely chopped fresh tarragon.

APRICOT ICE-CREAM (Serves about 8)

A sumptuous ice-cream, richly flavoured with Cointreau and studded with almonds.

8 oz. apricot jam (¾ to 1 cup) strained juice of 1 small lemon
1 liqueur-glass Cointreau
1 dozen blanched, toasted and finely chopped almonds

¼ pint double cream (2 cups whipping cream)
3 tablespoons milk

Set refrigerator control to lowest setting. Wash and dry 2 ice-cube trays. Put jam into bowl and mix thoroughly with strained lemon juice, Cointreau and almonds. Beat cream and milk together until just thick. Gently fold into apricot mixture and stir lightly until well combined. Transfer to prepared trays and leave in freezing compartment of refrigerator (or deep freeze) until ice-cream has frozen about ½ inch round sides of trays. Tip out into a chilled bowl and stir gently, without beating, until smooth. Pour back into trays, return to freezing compartment and freeze until firm. Spoon into dishes and serve with wafer biscuits.

ZABAGLIONE (Serves 4)

4 egg-yolks
2 oz. sifted icing sugar (just over ½ cup confectioner's sugar)

3 tablespoons Marsala (or Madeira can be used)

Put egg-yolks and sugar into a large bowl standing over a saucepan of gently simmering water, making sure base of bowl is not touching the water. Beat with a balloon whisk until mixture is light and foamy. Gradually add Marsala and continue beating until mixture is very thick, pale in colour and about twice its original volume. Pour into wineglasses and serve straight away with crisp, sweet biscuits.

Note: If a lighter, frothier Zabaglione is preferred, fold in 1 or 2 egg-whites, beaten to a stiff snow.

CRÈME CARAMEL (Serves 4)

3 level tablespoons granulated sugar
2 tablespoons hot water
1 dessertspoon boiling water
3 eggs

½ pint fresh or evaporated milk (1¼ cups)
1 tablespoon caster sugar
1 teaspoon vanilla essence

Well butter 4 individual metal moulds. Put sugar and hot water into a saucepan and leave over a low heat, stirring, until sugar dissolves. Bring to boil and boil steadily, without stirring, until syrup deepens in colour and turns a rich gold. Remove from heat and stir in boiling water. Very carefully (because hot caramel can give nasty burns) pour equal amounts into moulds. With the hand protected by an oven glove or cloth, tilt moulds in all directions so that the base and part of the sides of each get covered with caramel. Beat eggs and milk well together. Add sugar and vanilla and stir thoroughly. Strain into prepared moulds. Stand moulds in a baking dish containing about 1 inch of cold water. Put into centre of moderate oven (325°F. or Gas No. 3) and cook 30 to 40 minutes or until set. Leave until completely cold then refrigerate. Unmould before serving and accompany with single cream (coffee cream).

CHOCOLATE WHISKY MOUSSE (Serves 4)

4 oz. plain chocolate (4 squares)
2 oz. butter (¼ cup)
4 eggs, separated
2 tablespoons whisky
single cream (coffee cream)

Break up chocolate and put, with butter, into a large bowl or basin standing over a pan of hot (but not boiling) water. Leave until melted, stirring occasionally. Beat in egg-yolks and whisky. Whisk egg-whites to a stiff snow. Gently fold into chocolate mixture with a large metal spoon. When smooth and no longer streaky, transfer to 4 individual soufflé dishes, custard cups or wineglasses. Refrigerate overnight. Serve with a small jug of cream for pouring over the top of each. Thin, crisp biscuits make a pleasant accompaniment.

COUPE ADELINA PATTI (Serves 4)

16 to 20 *glacé* cherries
2 to 3 tablespoons brandy
sufficient vanilla ice-cream for
4 servings
4 tablespoons stiffly whipped cream

Put cherries into a small dish. Add brandy and cover with foil. Leave to soak overnight. Before serving, fill 4 individual glasses with ice-cream. Add 4 or 5 cherries, plus brandy, to each. Decorate by piping a large whirl of cream on top of each.

BRANDIED ORANGES (Serves 4)

4 large oranges
8 oz. granulated sugar
(approximately 1 cup)

¼ pint water (⅔ cup) for syrup
3 dessertspoons brandy

Put oranges into large bowl and cover with boiling water. Leave 15 minutes. (This makes them much easier to peel.) Drain thoroughly and cut skin into about 8 segments from top to bottom of each orange. Peel away and reserve skin of 2 oranges. Cut each orange *horizontally* into 4 or 5 slices. Put back together again and stand oranges, side by side, in a shallow serving-dish. Refrigerate. Take reserved segments of skin and cut away pith. Slice remaining skin into fine shreds and put into saucepan. Cover with water and simmer very gently, with lid on pan, for 30 minutes or until tender. Drain thoroughly. Put sugar and water into a saucepan. Bring to boil, stirring, and continue to boil gently until sugar has dissolved. Add shredded orange peel and brandy and cook gently until transparent; 5 to 10 minutes depending on heat. Cool to lukewarm then spoon syrup over oranges in dish. Take the orange skin and pile equal amounts on top of each orange. Chill at least 3 hours then serve with lightly whipped cream.

CHAMPAGNE CUP (Serves about 8)

Squeeze the juice of 1 small lemon into a large jug or bowl. Add 2 level tablespoons sifted icing sugar (confectioner's sugar), 2 liqueur glasses of Curaçao or brandy, about ½ pint (1¼ cups) soda water and 6 very thin slices of unpeeled cucumber. Add 1 bottle chilled champagne, 2 tablespoons crushed ice, 6 sliced strawberries, 1 unpeeled and thinly sliced orange and a few fresh mint leaves. Stir well to mix and pour into champagne glasses.

TIA MARIA CREAM (Serves 1)

A distant relation of Irish Coffee and a fine ending to a perfect meal.

Pour a liqueur glass of Tia Maria into a warm coffee cup (not too small). Two-thirds fill with freshly made strong coffee then top up with double cream (whipping cream) by pouring it into the cup over the back of a teaspoon. Serve straight away.

Scorpio

Scorpio

THE SCORPION — 23rd October to 21st November

RULING PLANET — MARS

Better by far you should forget and smile
Than that you should remember and be sad.

Christina Georgina Rossetti

Character Study — Nearly all Scorpionians are striking to look at, with intense, watchful and almost hypnotic eyes, thick hair—often coarse and curly—sensuous mouths, strong jaw-lines and aquiline noses. They have large broad heads, square faces, and often there is a gap between the two front teeth. They are generally big-boned, strongly built and muscular and can be either average in height or taller. In middle age, Scorpionians have a tendency to stoutness. The personality of the Scorpionian is magnetic, compelling, powerful and complex, with unmistakable traits of character which make him either liked or disliked. They are proud and dignified, penetrating critics and able judges. They have extraordinary determination, tenacity and self-control, with inborn courage, discretion, shrewdness, tact, intuition and caution. They are secretive and introspective, fascinated by mystery, and are great probers—getting to the heart of the matter is something they all try to do. They are idealistic, courageous, intellectual, ambitious, energetic, highly sensitive, sensual, moody, witty, emotional, passionate and possessive, and in their personal relationships with others can be intensely jealous, very suspicious, mistrustful and exacting. Nearly all Scorpionians are self-willed, outspoken, extremely good organizers, generous, interesting and sympathetic friends and exciting lovers. They are never dull, and although they are perfectionists on their own account they do not expect or demand the same perfection from others and have a surprising amount of tolerance and understanding. Sometimes Scorpionians are erratic, sceptical, obstinate, sarcastic, vindictive and revengeful, and with their long memories can make bitter and unforgiving enemies if they have been in some way wronged or crossed.

Marriage and children are important considerations to Scorpionians and to get maximum understanding, affection and loyalty from their partners, they should marry their fellow water signs, Cancerians or Pisceans. They are also compatible with the steadier Virgonians and Taureans but should avoid powerful Leonians (there would be a permanent clash of wills and temperament) and Aquarians.

Healing powers have been ascribed to Scorpionians and indeed a good number are strongly drawn to all branches of the medical profession and make conscientious, highly skilled and often brilliant physicians, surgeons, dentists, psychologists, psychiatrists and nurses. Those who do not take up medicine are equally successful in politics, the diplomatic service, research, electronics and engineering. Others become detectives (a most appropriate occupation for the analytical mind of the Scorpionian), chemists, actors and musicians.

Scorpionians are tough, with strong constitutions, and have considerable resistance to disease. They are, however, susceptible to atmosphere and environment, and can become sad and withdrawn if surrounded by unsympathetic and cold people. Anxiety and worry also make Scorpionians tense and nervous, resulting in irritability and sleeplessness.

Cooking — All Scorpionians enjoy good living and good eating and love food with a touch of mystery and originality. Whereas many of the other signs want to know exactly what it is they are eating and are suspicious of 'done-up' cooking, Scorpionians prefer their food to be novel and exotic, and adore spicy and often foreign dishes with interesting sauces and unusual trimmings and accompaniments.

Likes—Scorpionians like dramatic colours and in particular all shades of red from rich burgundy to deep pink. They love all that is new in fashion and are always prepared to experiment with bold ideas in clothes. They like exotic house-plants, tropical fish tanks, entertaining large numbers of people at once, impulsive trips, large cars, admiration from family and friends, holidays which are both restful and educational, visiting the theatre and opera, a comfortable home with antique and modern furniture combined, interior *décor* in rich colours and gifts of books—thrillers, crime and science fiction—good quality ornaments, cut glass, attractive china, jewellery and toiletries.

Dislikes — Scorpionians resent being forced into doing anything against their will, dislike wasting money (they tend to be penny wise and pound foolish), and become irritable with tradespeople and sales assistants if they are at all slow, unco-operative or just do not happen to stock the particular article required. Party-going they can take or leave depending on mood, they are intolerant of disobedience both in their own and other people's children and dieting publicly embarrasses them; they prefer to lose weight quietly and secretly without other people knowing.

Birth Stones — The birth stones for Scorpionians are the golden-brown topaz and green malachite streaked with copper. Topaz is mined in Brazil and the largest one in existence is in the Portuguese Crown Jewels. Malachite is a semi-precious stone which originally came from Russia. It is surrounded by rather charming folklore and, according to legend, it could make dwarfs and goblins invisible and enable a man to understand the language of the animals—provided he drank his wine from a malachite beaker! As an ornamental stone it is used mainly in rings, bracelets and brooches.

SCORPIO RECIPES

CHICKEN AND MUSHROOM COCKTAIL (Serves 6 as an *hors-d'œuvre*)

An interesting combination, with raw mushrooms adding a surprise touch.

8 oz. cold cooked chicken (2 cups)	1 tablespoon lemon juice
4 oz. sliced raw mushrooms (1¼ cups)	2 teaspoons Worcestershire sauce
¼ pint mayonnaise or salad cream (⅔ cup)	2 teaspoons horseradish sauce
4 tablespoons tomato ketchup	1 level teaspoon paprika shredded lettuce leaves
	4 lemon slices

Cut chicken into small cubes. Put into bowl with mushrooms and toss lightly together to mix. Beat mayonnaise or salad cream with ketchup, lemon juice, Worcestershire and horseradish sauces and paprika. Half fill 4 large wineglasses with lettuce. Add equal amounts of chicken and mushroom mixture to each then coat with the mayonnaise sauce. Add a lemon slice to each for garnish.

MELON COCKTAIL (Serves 8 to 10 as a starter)

1 large ripe melon (such as Honeydew)
caster sugar

juice of 2 large lemons
1 bottle dry white wine, chilled

Cut flesh of melon into small cubes and put into large serving-bowl. Sprinkle with caster sugar and the lemon juice. Toss well to mix, cover and refrigerate for 3 hours. Just before serving, stir in wine and ladle into bowls (melon and liquor together). Serve very cold.

CHEESE, LEEK AND PARSLEY SOUP (Serves 4 to 6)

3 tablespoons butter
2 medium chopped leeks (very well washed first)
4 level tablespoons flour
1 level teaspoon prepared mustard
2 pints milk (approximately 5 cups)

6 oz. grated cheddar cheese (approximately 2 cups)
1 teaspoon Worcestershire sauce
salt to taste
3 level tablespoons finely chopped parsley
1 extra tablespoon butter
3 level tablespoons fresh white breadcrumbs

Heat the 3 tablespoons of butter in saucepan. Add leeks and fry gently until soft but not brown. Stir in flour and mustard and cook for 2 minutes without browning. Gradually blend in milk. Cook, stirring, until soup comes to boil and thickens. Cover and simmer 10 minutes. Remove from heat, add cheese and stir until melted. Season with Worcestershire sauce and salt, add parsley and return to the lowest possible heat to keep hot. Melt extra butter in small pan. Add breadcrumbs and fry slowly until golden. Ladle soup into 4 or 6 soup cups or large bowls and sprinkle the top of each with fried crumbs. Serve very hot.

CHICKEN IN CREAM SAUCE WITH GRAPES
(Serves 4)

4 joints (about 2½ lb.) roasting chicken
3 tablespoons flour
½ teaspoon celery salt
1 teaspoon paprika
¼ teaspoon dry mustard
2 oz. margarine (¼ cup)
1 medium finely chopped onion (½ cup)
6 tablespoons dry sherry (½ cup)

6 tablespoons chicken stock (½ cup)
large pinch of dried tarragon
3 tablespoons mayonnaise (¼ cup)
1 carton soured cream (½ cup dairy soured cream)
2 tablespoons finely chopped parsley
4 oz. seedless green grapes*

Cut each joint into 2 pieces. Put flour into paper or polythene bag with celery salt, paprika and mustard. Add chicken, a few pieces at a time, and shake well to coat. (Hold bag firmly at the top while you are doing this.) Melt margarine in a heavy pan. Add chicken and fry until crisp on all sides. Remove to plate. Add onion to remaining margarine in pan and fry gently until soft and pale gold. Stir in any left-over flour from bag then pour in sherry and stock. Slowly bring to boil, stirring. Replace chicken and add tarragon. Lower heat and cover. Simmer gently until chicken is tender: about 45 minutes to 1 hour. Lift chicken onto warm serving dish. Stir mayonnaise, soured cream, parsley and grapes into pan juices. Heat through without boiling. Pour over chicken. Serve with freshly boiled rice or noodles.

* You can substitute ordinary grapes for seedless but halve first and remove pips.

WHISKY-BRAISED BEEF (Serves 6)

While searching for a change from Bœuf Bourguignonne, I experimented with whisky instead of red wine and this recipe is the result. It has a subtle warm flavour, and is eminently suitable for elegant dinner parties and family celebrations.

4 dessertspoons salad oil
2 medium finely chopped
  onions (1 cup)
3 lb. braising beef, cut into
  1-inch cubes
2 level dessertspoons flour

¼ pint water or beef stock
  (⅔ cup)
3 to 4 tablespoons whisky
3 tablespoons tomato *purée*
  garlic and ordinary salt to
  taste
freshly ground black pepper

Heat oil in large stewpan or skillet. Add onions. Fry gently, with lid on pan, until pale gold and soft. Add cubes of beef. Increase heat. Fry briskly until well browned, turning meat frequently. Stir in flour. Gradually pour in water or stock followed by whisky, *purée*, garlic and ordinary salt to taste and a grinding or two of black pepper. Bring to boil, stirring continuously. Lower heat and cover pan. Simmer very gently for 2 to 2½ hours or until meat is tender. Serve with cooked baby carrots and broad beans tossed in butter, and whole boiled potatoes sprinkled with parsley.

CIDER-BAKED STUFFED GAMMON ROLLS
(Serves 6)

1 medium onion
1 medium cooking apple
8 canned apricot halves
2 oz. butter (¼ cup)
2 tablespoons water
3 oz. fresh white breadcrumbs
  (approximately 2¼ cups)

½ level teaspoon marjoram
  salt and pepper to taste
6 large gammon rashers
¼ pint (⅔ cup) dry cider
  (apple cider)

Chop onion, the peeled and cored apple and apricot halves. Fry gently in the butter, with lid on pan, until soft: about 10 minutes. Add water and simmer a further 10 minutes. Remove from heat and stir in breadcrumbs and marjoram. Season to taste with salt and pepper (watch the salt: the gammon itself may be salty) then leave to cool. Spread each gammon rasher with an equal amount of stuffing, roll up and secure with cocktail sticks. Transfer to greased, fairly shallow casserole dish and add the cider. Cover closely with lid or aluminium foil and bake in centre of moderately hot oven (375°F. or Gas No. 5) for 30 minutes. Serve with baked jacket potatoes and a cooked green vegetable.

CURRIED TUNA (Serves 4)

2 oz. butter or margarine
(¼ cup)
2 teaspoons salad oil
2 large chopped onions
(approximately 2 cups)
1 garlic clove, very finely
chopped
1 large cooking apple
3 medium skinned tomatoes
1½ to 2 level tablespoons curry
powder

1 level tablespoon flour
1 level tablespoon tomato *purée*
2 teaspoons sugar
2 level tablespoons seedless
raisins
1 level teaspoon salt
½ pint chicken stock or water
(1¼ cups)
2 cans (each about 7 oz.) tuna

Heat butter or margarine and oil in saucepan. Add onions and garlic and fry gently, with lid on pan, until soft and golden; about 7 minutes. Chop apple and tomatoes. Add to pan and fry a further 5 minutes. Stir in curry powder, flour, tomato *purée*, sugar, raisins and salt. Gradually blend in stock or water. Cook, stirring, until mixture comes to boil and thickens. Lower heat and cover pan. Simmer *very gently* for 45 minutes, stirring occasionally. About 10 minutes before sauce is ready, remove tuna from cans and separate into chunks. Add to pan and heat through a further 5 to 7 minutes. Accompany with freshly boiled rice (allowing 2 to 3 oz. raw weight per person) and small side-dishes of desiccated coconut, thinly sliced cucumber, chutney and natural yogurt.

COFFEE-BASTED ROAST LAMB (Serves 8 to 10)

One of the most exotic and exciting recipes for lamb I've ever come across. It was tried out on me at a dinner party about two years ago and I have been surprising my own guests with it ever since!

1 large leg of lamb (about 6 lb.)
2 large garlic cloves, peeled and
sliced
½ level teaspoon powdered
ginger

¼ pint hot strong coffee (⅔ cup)
2 teaspoons brown sugar
2 tablespoons evaporated milk
4 tablespoons dry red wine
3 level tablespoons flour

1 level teaspoon dry mustard
½ level teaspoon powdered
    cinnamon

3 level tablespoons red-currant
jelly
seasoning to taste

Make several slits in the lamb and insert the slices of garlic. Mix together ginger, mustard and cinnamon and sprinkle over lamb, covering entire surface. Stand meat on rack in large roasting tin. Put into centre of moderate oven (350°F. or Gas No. 4) and roast for 1½ hours. Combine coffee with sugar, milk and wine. Pour over lamb. Return to oven and continue to roast for a further 1½ hours, basting meat with coffee liquid at least 3 more times. Transfer meat to a carving board and keep hot. Pour lamb and coffee juices into a measuring cup and make up to ¾ pint (2 cups) with hot water. Stir flour into dish in which lamb was roasted. Cook, stirring, for 2 minutes. Gradually blend in the ¾ pint juices. Cook, stirring all the time, until sauce comes to boil and thickens. Add red-currant jelly and simmer a further 5 minutes. Adjust seasoning to taste and pour into a large, warm gravy boat. Serve with the lamb.

PORK CHOPS IN VERMOUTH (Serves 4)

4 pork chops, each weighing
    about 6 oz.
¼ pint dry vermouth (⅔ cup)
¼ pint salad oil (⅔ cup)
1 medium chopped onion
    (½ cup)
1 tablespoon lemon juice

1 level teaspoon finely grated
    orange peel
1 level teaspoon garlic salt
    (or plain salt if preferred)
½ teaspoon dried sage
    freshly milled black pepper

Cut surplus fat away from chops. Stand chops in shallow glass or enamel dish. Beat vermouth with oil, onion, lemon juice, orange peel, garlic salt and sage. Season with freshly milled pepper then pour over chops. Cover and refrigerate for a minimum of 4 hours, turning at least 3 times. Transfer to grill-pan and grill 18 to 20 minutes, turning frequently and brushing liberally with the vermouth mixture.

BEEF—MARENGO STYLE (Serves 4)

2 to 2½ lb. stewing beef
3 level tablespoons flour
1 oz. butter (⅛ cup)
1 tablespoon olive or salad oil
1 large chopped onion
  (approximately 1 cup)
1 garlic clove, chopped
2 level tablespoons tomato
  purée
½ pint dry red wine (1¼ cups)

4 large skinned and chopped
  tomatoes
1 to 2 level teaspoons salt
2 level teaspoons sugar
1 bay leaf
3 heaped tablespoons finely
  chopped parsley
2 dozen stoned black olives
4 oz. sliced mushrooms
  (1¼ cups)
1 liqueur glass brandy

Cut beef into 1-inch cubes and coat with flour. Heat butter and oil in saucepan. Add onion and garlic and fry, with lid on pan, until soft and pale gold. Add beef cubes (and any loose flour) and fry a little more briskly until surfaces are brown and well sealed. Stir in *purée*, wine, tomatoes, salt, sugar and bay leaf. Bring to boil, stirring. Lower heat, cover pan and simmer gently for 2¼ hours. Add parsley, olives and mushrooms. Pour brandy into ladle and flame. When flames have subsided, add to pan. Simmer a further 15 to 30 minutes or until beef is tender. Serve with freshly boiled rice and a large green salad.

TRIPE LYONNAISE (Serves 4)

2 lb. dressed tripe
2 oz. butter or margarine
  (¼ cup)
2 large chopped onions
  (approximately 2 cups)

3 level tablespoons flour
¾ pint hot chicken stock
  (2 cups)
salt and pepper to taste

Wash tripe well and cut into 2-inch squares. Heat butter or margarine in a large saucepan. Add onions and fry slowly until deep gold. Add flour and continue to cook, stirring all the time, until they brown lightly. Gradually blend in stock then bring to boil, stirring continuously. Add tripe and seasoning to taste, cover pan and simmer 35 to 40 minutes or until tender, stirring occasionally to prevent sticking. Serve with creamy mashed potatoes and a cooked green vegetable.

BLUE-CHEESE-STUFFED POTATOES (Serves 4)

4 large potatoes	6 tablespoons soured cream
salad oil	(dairy soured cream)
1 tablespoon butter	1 level teaspoon prepared
4 oz. blue-vein cheese (Danish	mustard
Blue or Stilton), crumbled	salt and pepper to taste
	paprika

Wash and scrub potatoes and prick skins all over with a fork. Brush lightly with oil then transfer to baking tray. Cook in centre of moderately hot oven (375°F. or Gas No. 5) for about 2 hours or until potatoes feel soft when lightly pressed between fingers. Remove from oven and cut a slice off the top of each. Scoop insides into bowl and mash finely. Beat until creamy with the butter, cheese, 4 tablespoons of the soured cream, mustard and salt and pepper to taste. Return to potato cases, trickle remaining cream over the top of each and dust lightly with paprika. Re-heat towards top of hot oven (425°F. or Gas No. 7) for 10 minutes.

FLEMISH STYLE CARROTS (Serves 4 to 6)

1½ lb. new carrots	2 egg-yolks
1 tablespoon butter	4 tablespoons double cream
1 level teaspoon caster sugar	(whipping cream)
4 tablespoons water	1 level tablespoon finely
¼ level teaspoon salt	chopped parsley

Cover carrots with boiling water. Drain, rinse under cold water and scrape off skins. Cut into slices about ⅛ inch in thickness and put into saucepan with butter, sugar, water and salt. Cover and simmer 20 minutes, shaking pan frequently to prevent browning. Beat yolks and cream well together. Add to carrots with parsley and stir over the lowest possible heat until mixture thickens, but under no circumstances allow it to boil. Serve straight away with poultry, roasts and grills or with poached fish dishes.

CHESTNUT SAUCE (Serves about 6)

A chunky, well-flavoured sauce-cum-gravy that teams perfectly with turkey or chicken.

4 dozen dried chestnuts	2 teaspoons butter
1 wineglass dry white wine	$\frac{1}{4}$ level teaspoon powdered
turkey or chicken stock	nutmeg

Soak chestnuts overnight in cold water. Drain and put into saucepan with wine, stock just to cover, butter and nutmeg. Bring to boil and lower heat. Cover and simmer until chestnuts are tender but still whole. Lift out of saucepan with perforated spoon and transfer to a large gravy boat. Boil chestnut liquor very briskly for a few minutes to reduce it by approximately one third. Pour over the chestnuts and serve straight away.

CRÈME SUISSE (Serves 6)

An unusual dessert—which is a cross between ice-cream and frozen mousse—temptingly flavoured with Grand Marnier and rum.

4 large eggs, separated	$\frac{1}{4}$ pint double cream ($\frac{2}{3}$ cup
3 oz. caster sugar	whipping cream)
(approximately $\frac{3}{8}$ cup)	3 tablespoons Grand Marnier
6 oz. cream cheese	

Fruit Sauce

5 dessertspoons brown rum	1 level tablespoon mixed
4 tablespoons water	chopped peel
3 level tablespoons seedless	2 level tablespoons chopped
raisins	*glacé* cherries

Beat egg-yolks and sugar together until very thick, pale in colour and at least twice their original volume. Whisk in the cheese and continue to whisk until mixture is smooth. Beat cream until thick and fold into cheese mixture with Grand Marnier and stiffly beaten egg-whites. Pour into one large empty ice-cube tray, or 2 smaller ones, and leave in freezing compartment of refrigerator for 6 to 8 hours. (Do not lower temperature as for ice-cream.)

To make sauce, bring rum and water just up to the boil. Add raisins and peel. Pour into bowl and refrigerate, covered, for the same length of time as the cheese mixture. Add cherries.

To serve, spoon equal amounts of Crème Suisse into 6 sundae glasses then coat with fruit sauce.

BUTTERSCOTCH PEACH SUNDAE (Serves 4)

4 large ripe peaches
2 tablespoons butter
3 tablespoons brown sugar
   juice of ½ lemon

4 thick slices of jam-filled Swiss roll (jelly roll)
4 heaped tablespoons vanilla ice-cream

Wash peaches and dry thoroughly. (Do not peel.) Cut into thin slices. Melt butter in frying-pan. Add sugar and cook gently until mixture bubbles. Add peach slices and cook until heated through and well glazed, turning them over from time to time with a spoon. Remove from heat and stir in lemon juice. Stand Swiss roll on 4 individual plates. Cover with peach slices and syrup then top each with a tablespoon of ice-cream. Serve straight away.

SPICED PEARS IN WINE (Serves 4)

4 large dessert pears
½ pint red wine (1¼ cups)
8 oz. caster sugar
   (approximately 1 cup)

1 cinnamon stick
4 cloves
1 lemon, thinly sliced
½ teaspoon vanilla essence

Peel, halve and core pears then stand in shallow heatproof dish. Put all remaining ingredients into saucepan. Bring to boil, stirring, and continue to cook until sugar has completely dissolved. Pour over pears. Cover dish with aluminium foil and bake in centre of moderate oven (350°F. or Gas No. 4) for 30 minutes. Uncover and bake a further 20 minutes, basting at least twice with wine syrup. Serve hot with syrup and thin sweet biscuits, or chill thoroughly and serve with whipped cream or ice-cream.

MULLED WINE (Serves 6)

1 cinnamon stick

1 blade mace

3 cloves

1 breakfast cup water

powdered nutmeg

1 pint port (2¼ cups)

sugar to taste

Put cinnamon stick, mace, cloves and water into a saucepan. Bring to boil and boil gently for 5 minutes. Add a little nutmeg then pour in the port. When very hot, add sugar to taste. Bring to boil and boil for 1 minute. Ladle into cups and serve very hot.

ICED TEA WITH BRANDY

An exquisitely refreshing drink for hot summer evenings.

For 4 to 6 persons, make up about 1½ pints (about 4 cups) of tea a little stronger than usual and strain into a jug. Add a sliced lemon, 6 fresh mint leaves, a 4-inch length of orange peel and sugar to taste. Stir well to combine, leave tea until completely cold, then strain. Take 4 large tumblers and put 3 to 4 ice-cubes and a tot of brandy into each. Fill with cold tea and drink through straws. If liked, a slice of fresh lemon or orange may be added to each glass before serving.

BANANA CHUTNEY

A distinctive, spicy and uncommon chutney which should appeal strongly to all Scorpionians. It goes very well indeed with poultry grills and roasts, grilled or fried gammon and roast pork.

1 dozen large bananas

6 large skinned tomatoes

3 large onions

1 garlic clove

8 oz. brown sugar

(approximately 1⅛ cups)

8 oz. seedless raisins

(approximately 1⅜ cups)

1 green pepper

½ pint malt vinegar (1¼ cups)

2 level teaspoons salt

4 cloves

1 small bay leaf

Chop bananas, tomatoes, onions and garlic. Put into saucepan with sugar and raisins. Halve green pepper, remove inside fibres and seeds and chop flesh finely. Add to saucepan with all remaining ingredients. Bring slowly to boil then simmer very gently, uncovered, until chutney is thick and the same consistency as jam. Transfer to warm dry jars when lukewarm and cover when completely cold.

Sagittarius

Sagittarius

THE ARCHER — 22nd November to 20th December

RULING PLANET — JUPITER

For my part, I travel not to go anywhere, but to go.
I travel for travel's sake. The great affair is to move.
Robert Louis Stevenson

Character Study — Sagittarians are usually taller than average with long, firm limbs and large hands and feet. They carry themselves upright with dignity and poise and can be very handsome people, with frank, expressive and bright eyes—in blue, hazel or velvety brown—high foreheads, oval faces, well-shaped eyebrows and attractive noses which are sometimes snubbed or tip-tilted. They have fresh, healthy-looking complexions with thick and often naturally curly hair ranging in colour from dark auburn to brunette. People of this group are generous, kind, sympathetic, charitable, reasonable, strong-willed, faithful, discreet, extremely good organizers, independent, very idealistic, imaginative, candid and highly ambitious. They are humane, with a strong sense of justice, and any harshness meted out to others (and especially if it is directed towards their own family, friends and acquaintances) amounts, in their eyes, to a personal attack on themselves. They are sensitive, almost touchy, and many respond badly to criticism even when it is constructive and well-meaning. They are optimistic, impulsive, versatile, very active and enterprising, with an inborn love of liberty, freedom of speech and truth. Nevertheless they do not always trust people around them (they occasionally doubt even themselves) and this leads to the two very things they want most to avoid: deception and hypocrisy. In general, Sagittarians are thinkers. They are quick at learning, quick at assimilating and they have a deep interest in all research and study, especially if it is connected with philosophy, politics and religion. They make good friends, rarely betraying a confidence, faithful and loving partners and kind parents, and thoroughly enjoy being surrounded by companionable people, particularly if they are bright and intelligent with original ideas and thoughts. Sagittarians can be restless, easily bored with routine, rebellious, secretive, diffuse and indifferent and can also display petulance, impatience and brusqueness when roused to anger or self-defence. Consequently they appear complex and difficult to understand, and the fact that they are changeable in their views and opinions only adds to the enigma. They nearly all crave change and this makes them ardent and frequent travellers; it is a fact that many of this sign have such a wanderlust that they often emigrate and start a completely new life in a foreign country. The early part of a Sagittarian's life may be upset by obstacles and family problems, but the latter half should be tempered with a good deal more calm and happiness.

They usually have good health but are prone to upper respiratory infections, varicose veins and rheumatism and sciatica in the hips and thighs. Round about the thirty-year mark, Sagittarians sometimes have nervous breakdowns or very severe bouts of depression caused, in many cases, from overwork and excessive worry.

In marriage they are happiest, and indeed most fortunate, with Librans, Leonians, Arieans and sometimes their direct opposite: the Geminians. They are out of harmony with earthy Virgonians and watery Pisceans.

Those Sagittarians who choose the professions make excellent teachers, lecturers, politicians and lawyers. Others are drawn to music, journalism and writing, advertising, public relations, religious and philanthropic movements, banking, the clothing industry, shipping and the services.

Cooking — Sagittarians have hearty appetites and love food, preferring down-to-earth bistro style dishes from all over the globe to anything very elaborate and formal. This group are the casserole, stew, soup and vegetable fans and are much more content with an outsize hot-pot containing everything under the sun than an elegant and classic *haute cuisine* dish.

Likes — Sagittarians like all the browns from warm beige to dark coffee, all shades of green and blue and sometimes purple. They feel comfortable in casual clothes provided they are well-cut and elegant, with the addition of bold accessories and pieces of chunky jewellery. They love being out in the fresh air and enjoy outdoor sports, such as skiing, riding, golf, swimming, tennis and walking. Most Sagittarians are fond of flowering shrubs, evergreen bushes and indoor plants, animals, conversation, amateur dramatics and operatics, going to and giving parties, budgeting, small economical cars, active holidays, long weekends away, helping the community, and practical gifts both of a personal nature and for the home, including scarves, sweaters, ties, purses, wallets, pens, pencils, toiletries, jewellery, indoor plants, table-ware, bathroom and kitchen accessories and car gadgets. Little Sagittarians will always appreciate a pet of their own, cuddly toys, nature books, tricycles and bicycles, puzzles and illustrated story-books about travel and adventure.

Dislikes — Sagittarians dislike spending money on themselves, too much formality, having to make snap decisions, driving for the sake of driving and being alone for any length of time; all Sagittarians like and need the company of people. They hate being exploited in any way and are irritated by those who are less reliable than themselves.

Birth Stone — The birth stone for Sagittarians is a zircon, a gem which, when clear, closely resembles the diamond in appearance, although it is much less hard. The blue zircons and the clear ones as well begin life as yellow-brownish stones. They are then heat-treated and subsequently turn a beautiful aquamarine colour or become clear and diamond-like. Zircons come from the East and are connected with wisdom, intellect, success, good luck and happiness.

SAGITTARIUS RECIPES

BOLOGNESE PANCAKES (Serves 8 as an *hors-d'œuvre*; 4 as a main course)

This one is especially for lovers of Italian food. The big advantage here is that both the pancakes and the Bolognese sauce can be made a day beforehand, leaving just a tiny bit of last-minute preparation.

Bolognese Sauce

3 dessertspoons salad oil
2 medium finely chopped onions
(approximately 1 cup)
1 peeled and chopped garlic
clove
1 lb. raw minced beef
3 tablespoons tomato *purée*

2 level dessertspoons flour
½ pint water (1¼ cups)
½ to 1 level teaspoon salt
1 level teaspoon sugar
½ level teaspoon dried basil or
mixed herbs

Cheese Sauce

1 oz. butter (⅛ cup)
2 level tablespoons flour
½ pint milk (1¼ cups)

3 oz. grated cheddar cheese
(approximately 1 cup)
salt, pepper and mustard to
taste

To assemble pancakes

8 cooked pancakes
8 tablespoons stock or dry
white wine

2 tablespoons tomato ketchup
2 oz. grated cheddar cheese
(approximately ⅔ cup)

To make Bolognese sauce, heat oil in saucepan. Add onion and garlic and fry gently until golden. Add minced beef and fry briskly until well browned, stirring with a fork all the time. Add all remaining ingredients. Mix well and slowly bring to boil. Cover and simmer very gently for 45 minutes, stirring occasionally.

To make cheese sauce (which should be done about 10 minutes before assembling pancakes) melt butter in saucepan, stir in flour and cook without browning for 2 minutes. Gradually blend in milk. Bring sauce slowly to boil, stirring or whisking gently all the time. Simmer 2 minutes then add cheese. Season to taste with salt, pepper and mustard. Leave over a very low heat.

Fill pancakes with equal amounts of hot Bolognese sauce. (If previously made, boil it gently for at least 10 minutes.) Roll up and arrange in heatproof dish. Moisten with stock or wine then coat with hot cheese sauce. Trickle ketchup over top then sprinkle with cheese. Re-heat and brown towards top of hot oven (425°F. or Gas No. 7) for about 15 minutes.

Note: If pancakes have been made a day before, stack them in an air-tight tin with greaseproof paper between each. Cover tin with lid and store in the refrigerator.

SOUP BONNE FEMME (Serves 6)

1 small cucumber	2 pints chicken stock (5 cups)
1 medium sized lettuce	salt and pepper to taste
2 oz. butter ($\frac{1}{4}$ cup)	2 egg-yolks
2 level tablespoons flour	$\frac{1}{4}$ pint double cream ($\frac{2}{3}$ cup
3 tablespoons cold milk	whipping cream)

Peel cucumber and grate coarsely. Wash lettuce, shake leaves dry, then cut into thin shreds. Heat butter in a large saucepan. Add cucumber and lettuce and cook very gently, with lid on pan, for 10 minutes. Mix flour to a smooth cream with the cold milk. Combine with stock then pour into saucepan. Cook, stirring, until soup comes to boil and thickens, then season to taste with salt and pepper. Lower heat, cover and simmer 15 minutes. Remove from heat. Beat egg-yolks and cream well together then blend in some of the hot soup. Return to saucepan, stir well and serve straight away.

PANADE (Serves 4)

A warming and flavourful bread-thickened soup from France.

1 tablespoon butter	salt and pepper to taste
2 medium finely chopped onions (1 cup)	$\frac{1}{4}$ pint plus 3 tablespoons milk (1 cup)
1 pint chicken stock ($2\frac{1}{2}$ cups)	1 large egg
3 large slices diced bread (3 cups)	chopped parsley

Heat butter in large, heavy pan. Add onions. Cover pan and cook gently until soft and pale gold; about 10 minutes. Stir in stock and bread. Season to taste with salt and pepper. Simmer 30 minutes. Whisk with hand-whisk until smooth. Beat milk and egg well together. Add a little hot soup. Pour back into saucepan. Re-heat without boiling. Pour into soup bowls and sprinkle parsley over each. Serve while still very hot.

BARLEY BEEF BROTH (Serves 6 to 8)

1 lb. shin of beef
2 pints water (5 cups)
2 medium sliced onions
5 level tablespoons well-washed
   pearl barley

a handful of coarsely chopped
   parsley
1 teaspoon dried thyme
1 to 2 level teaspoons salt
   pepper to taste
6 potatoes

Cut beef into thin strips. Put into saucepan with water, onions, barley, parsley, thyme and salt and pepper to taste. Bring to boil slowly and remove scum. Lower heat and cover pan. Simmer very gently for 2½ hours. Peel potatoes and wash. Cut into thick slices and add to soup. Simmer a further 20 to 30 minutes. Ladle into warm soup bowls or plates and serve very hot.

DUTCH POTATO CASSEROLE (Serves 4)

1½ lb. cold cooked potatoes
3 large skinned tomatoes
1 large onion
2 tablespoons finely chopped
   parsley
6 oz. grated Gouda cheese
   (approximately 2 cups)

salt and pepper
2 level tablespoons cornflour
   (corn starch)
2 tablespoons cold milk
¼ pint hot stock (⅔ cup)

Cut potatoes into medium thick slices. Slice tomatoes fairly thinly. Coarsely grate onion. Chop parsley. Fill a 1½-pint buttered casserole dish with alternate layers of potato, tomato, onion, parsley and cheese, beginning with potato and ending with cheese and sprinkling salt and pepper between layers. Blend cornflour (corn starch) to a smooth cream with the cold milk then combine with hot stock. Gently pour into casserole. Bake, uncovered, in centre of moderately hot oven (375°F. or Gas No. 5) for 30 minutes.

HEAVEN AND EARTH (Serves 4)

An old German dish featuring calves' liver; the apples represent heaven, the potatoes, earth.

3 dessertspoons salad oil	extra butter
2 teaspoons butter	milk
3 medium chopped onions	salt and pepper to taste
(1½ cups)	½ pint apple sauce (1¼ cups)
1 lb. potatoes	4 slices calves' liver (each about 4 oz.)

Put oil and the butter into frying pan or skillet. Add onions. Cover and fry over a very low heat for about 30 minutes, shaking pan from time to time. Meanwhile peel the potatoes and cut into pieces. Cook in boiling salted water until tender. Drain and mash very finely with a large piece of butter. Beat to a light cream with milk then season to taste with salt and pepper. Leave over a low heat. Warm up apple sauce. Add slices of liver to pan of onions and fry briskly for 5 minutes, turning once. Arrange on serving-dish with onions and serve with the potatoes and warm apple sauce.

BŒUF EN DAUBE (Serves 4 generously)

A superior French beef stew with a memorable flavour.

2½ to 3 lb. lean stewing beef	2 tablespoons olive oil
4 oz. unsmoked bacon, bought in one piece	2 sprigs parsley
	1 sprig thyme
3 carrots	1 small bay leaf
3 medium onions	¼ pint dry red wine (⅔ cup)
3 large skinned tomatoes	salt and freshly milled pepper
2 garlic cloves	to taste

Cut meat into 1-inch cubes. Cut bacon into tiny dice. Peel carrots and onions and slice thinly. Chop tomatoes roughly. Chop garlic finely. Heat oil in a flameproof casserole. Add bacon, vegetables, and garlic. Fry gently for 5 minutes. Add meat cubes and cook 10 minutes over a moderate heat, turning frequently. Add parsley, thyme, bay leaf and red wine. Season to taste with salt and pepper. Bring to boil. Remove from heat and cover. Cook in centre of cool oven (300°F. or

Gas No. 2) for 3 to 3½ hours or until meat is tender. Serve with boiled potatoes or freshly cooked noodles tossed in butter. Accompany with a mixed green salad or cooked green vegetable.

HAMBURGER PIE (Serves 6)

6 oz. short-crust pastry made with 6 oz. flour (6 oz. pie pastry)
1 lb. lean minced beef
5 tablespoons evaporated milk
4 tablespoons tomato ketchup

1 oz. fresh white breadcrumbs (approximately ¾ cup)
1 small grated onion
½ level teaspoon basil
salt and pepper to taste
6 oz. sliced mushrooms (approximately 2 cups)
1 tablespoon butter

Roll out pastry and use to line an 8-inch lightly greased heatproof pie plate. Flute edges or ridge with fork to decorate. Combine beef with milk, ketchup, breadcrumbs, onion, basil and salt and pepper to taste. Mix thoroughly then spoon into pastry case. Spread top evenly with a knife then bake in centre of a moderately hot oven (375°F. or Gas No. 5) for 40 to 45 minutes or until pastry is pale gold and meat filling is firm. Remove from oven. Fry mushrooms in the butter for 5 minutes, spoon over top of pie and serve straight away.

SMOKED HADDOCK AND EGG CASSEROLE
(Serves 4 to 6)

1½ lb. smoked haddock fillet
6 hard-boiled eggs
2 oz. butter or margarine (¼ cup)
2 oz. flour (approximately ¼ cup)
1 pint milk (2½ cups)
1 tablespoon lemon juice

2 teaspoons Worcestershire sauce
½ level teaspoon prepared mustard
8 oz grated cheddar cheese (approximately 3 cups)
salt and pepper to taste
paprika

Poach smoked haddock in unsalted water until tender; 10 to 15 minutes depending on thickness. Drain. Flake up flesh with 2 forks, discarding skin and bones if any. Shell eggs and slice thinly. Melt butter or margarine in saucepan. Add flour and cook gently for 2 minutes without browning. Gradually blend in milk. Cook, stirring all the time, until sauce comes to boil and thickens. Simmer 2 minutes then stir in lemon juice, Worcestershire sauce, mustard and 6 oz. grated cheese. Season to taste with salt and pepper, bearing in mind that the fish will contribute its own saltiness. Fill a 2-pint buttered heatproof dish with alternate layers of fish, eggs and cheese sauce, ending with a layer of sauce. Sprinkle rest of cheese on top, add a light dusting of paprika and brown near top of moderately hot oven (375°F. or Gas No. 5) for 20 to 25 minutes. Serve with buttered green peas and baked tomato halves.

SUMMER LAMB STEW (Serves 4)

1 lb. fillet of lamb cut from leg
2 level tablespoons flour, well seasoned with salt and pepper
1 tablespoon oil or dripping
4 large skinned tomatoes
½ pint water (1¼ cups)
1 level teaspoon sugar

1 teaspoon Worcestershire sauce
1 level teaspoon chopped fresh mint
8 shallots or small onions
8 oz. sliced green beans
1 dozen new potatoes
seasoning to taste

Cut meat into 1-inch cubes and coat with seasoned flour. Heat oil or dripping in saucepan. Add meat cubes and fry briskly until well browned. Chop tomatoes and add to pan with water, sugar, Worcestershire sauce and mint. Cover and simmer for about 1¼ hours or until meat is just tender. Add all remaining ingredients, season to taste and cook a further 20 to 30 minutes.

FRUITED PORK HOT-POT (Serves 4)

1½ lb. fresh belly of pork, boned
2 level tablespoons flour, seasoned with salt and pepper
1 tablespoon dripping or oil
2 medium onions
1 pint water (2½ cups)
8 small carrots

8 potatoes
2 celery stalks
1 small turnip or parsnip
handful of finely chopped parsley
6 level tablespoons sweetcorn
2 large cooking apples

Cut meat into fairly large cubes and coat with seasoned flour. Heat dripping or oil in large flameproof casserole. Slice onions thinly, add to pan and fry until pale gold. Add pork cubes (and any loose flour) and fry a little more briskly until light brown and crisp. Pour in water and slowly bring to boil. Peel carrots and potatoes and leave whole. Cut celery into diagonal strips. Peel turnip or parsnip and cut into small cubes. Add prepared vegetables to casserole with parsley and sweet-corn. Peel apples and remove cores. Cut into fairly thick slices and add to casserole. Cover with lid or aluminium foil and cook in centre of cool oven (325°F. or Gas No. 3) for 3 hours.

VEAL CHASSEUR (Serves 4)

2 to 2½ lb. stewing veal	3 large skinned tomatoes, chopped
3 level tablespoons flour	
1 oz. butter (⅛ cup)	1 to 2 level teaspoons salt
1 tablespoon olive or salad oil	2 level teaspoons sugar
1 large chopped onion (approximately 1 cup)	1 bay leaf
	⅛ teaspoon dried thyme
1 garlic clove, chopped	¼ level teaspoon basil
4 level tablespoons tomato *purée*	4 oz. sliced mushrooms (1¼ cups)
½ pint dry white wine (1¼ cups)	
	1 liqueur glass brandy

Cut veal into 1 inch cubes and coat with flour. Heat butter and oil in large saucepan. Add onion and garlic and fry gently until soft and pale gold. Add veal (and any loose flour) and fry a little more briskly until all surfaces are brown and well sealed. Stir in *purée*, wine, tomatoes, salt, sugar, bay leaf, thyme and basil. Bring to boil, stirring. Cover pan and lower heat. Simmer gently for 1½ hours. Add mushrooms. Pour brandy into a ladle and flame. When flames have subsided pour into saucepan. Stir well and simmer a further 15 to 20 minutes or until veal is tender. Serve with freshly boiled flat ribbon noodles tossed with a little butter. Accompany with a green salad.

SPLIT PEA AND RICE KEDGEREE (Serves about 8)

A rather different version from the more usual one, but popular as a breakfast dish at the turn of the century along with a host of other Kedgerees (or Kadgiori, Kitcheeree and Kitcheree as they were some-times called) which we 'imported' from India and subsequently adopted.

½ lb. split peas
  (approximately 1 cup)
½ lb. long-grain rice
  (approximately 1 cup)
1 level teaspoon salt
½ level teaspoon powdered
  ginger

1 blade mace
1 oz. butter (⅛ cup)
2 teaspoons salad oil
2 large and thinly sliced onions
8 hard-boiled eggs, freshly
  cooked

Soak peas overnight in cold water. Drain and put into saucepan with rice, salt, ginger and mace. Add sufficient cold water to cover. Bring to boil and lower heat. Cook gently until peas and rice are both tender, adding a little extra boiling water if mixture seems to be too dry. Mean-while, heat butter and oil in a frying-pan. Add onions and fry gently until golden brown. Heap pea and rice mixture onto a platter (draining first if necessary and also removing blade of mace) then top with fried onions and any butter from pan. Shell and halve eggs and arrange round edge of platter. Serve hot.

RATATOUILLE WITH RICE (Sufficient for about 8 servings)

One of my favourite emergency stand-bys. I make a large quantity of Ratatouille when the vegetables needed for it are readily available and at their cheapest, and then deep freeze it in plastic bags or tubs. If I want a quick meal, I simply cook some long-grain rice, top it with hot Ratatouille and then sprinkle Parmesan cheese thickly over the top. It makes a simple but thoroughly appetizing and enjoyable meal and is the sort of thing one could give, quite happily, to unexpected guests.

2 large onions
2 garlic cloves
4 tablespoons salad oil
2 large aubergines (egg-plant)
1½ lb. marrow or courgettes

2 large green peppers
1½ lb. skinned tomatoes
1 to 2 level teaspoons salt
6 tablespoons finely chopped
  parsley

Slice onions very thinly. Chop garlic. Heat oil in large saucepan. Add onions and garlic and fry gently until pale gold. Meanwhile, wash aubergines, wipe dry and slice thinly. Peel marrow and cube, or cut unpeeled courgettes into ½-inch thick slices. Halve green peppers, remove seeds and fibres and cut flesh into thin strips. Coarsely chop tomatoes. Add all prepared vegetables to pan with salt and parsley then simmer gently, in covered pan, for 1 hour. Uncover and continue to cook a further 30 minutes or until mixture is quite thick and almost the consistency of jam.

CABBAGE CASSEROLE (Serves 4)

1 medium sized head of cabbage	1 tablespoon vinegar
12 oz. cold boiled bacon	5 tablespoons water
1 tablespoon dripping	6 parboiled potatoes
1 level tablespoon flour	3 skinned tomatoes

Wash outside of cabbage, removing any discoloured and damaged leaves. Cut in half from top to bottom then cut each half into 2 wedges (total of 4 wedges). Cut bacon into small cubes. Heat dripping in flameproof casserole and add bacon. Fry gently until golden then stir in flour. Cook for 2 minutes without browning. Gradually blend in vinegar and water. Bring to boil, stirring, then add wedges of cabbage. Slice potatoes thickly and coarsely chop tomatoes. Put both into casserole around cabbage. Cover with lid or aluminium foil and cook in centre of moderate oven (350°F. or Gas No. 4) for 1¼ to 1½ hours or until cabbage is tender.

SAILOR'S STYLE FISH RAGOUT (Serves 4 to 6)

1 lb. skinned and filleted haddock	cold water
	3 oz. butter (⅜ cup)
1 lb. skinned and filleted cod	1 dozen very small onions or shallots
1 thinly sliced onion	
1 level teaspoon mixed herbs	2 teaspoons salad oil
2 cloves	3 level tablespoons flour
1 wineglass dry white or red wine	2 dozen button mushrooms
	3 tablespoons chopped parsley

Cut both fish into large chunks. Put into saucepan with onion, herbs, cloves, wine and sufficient cold water just to cover. Bring to boil and lower heat. Cover pan and poach very gently for 20 minutes. Meanwhile, melt butter in a separate pan. Add onions or shallots and salad oil and fry gently until deep gold, turning frequently. Stir in flour, cook gently for 2 minutes and remove from heat. Strain fish liquor and reserve. Keep pieces of fish hot. Gradually add fish liquor to saucepan of onions. Cook, stirring, until mixture comes to boil and thickens. Add mushrooms, cover pan and simmer 10 minutes. Arrange fish on a warm platter. Coat with sauce, onions and mushrooms, sprinkle with parsley and serve while still very hot.

SWEDISH PORK SALAD (Serves 6)

1 medium sized lettuce
12 slices cold roast pork
½ pint thick mayonnaise
(1¼ cups)
¼ pint thick unsweetened
apple *purée* (⅔ cup)

1 level teaspoon grated horse-radish
½ a peeled cucumber
1 orange, cut into thin slices

Line a serving platter with lettuce then cover with slices of pork. Combine mayonnaise with apple *purée* and horse-radish and spoon over meat. Slice cucumber thinly and arrange round edge of platter. Garnish with the orange slices, each slit once from centre to outside edge and shaped into a twist.

SPANISH LUNCH SALAD (Serves 4)

4 large cooked potatoes
1 large cooked beetroot
1 large onion
6 canned artichoke hearts
4 large skinned tomatoes
1 dozen anchovy fillets
4 sliced hard-boiled eggs

1 dozen stuffed olives
6 tablespoons olive oil
salt and pepper
2 tablespoons lemon juice
1 tablespoon wine vinegar
1 tablespoon finely chopped parsley

Cut potatoes into dice and put into mixing-bowl. Cut beetroot into narrow strips. Peel and slice onion then separate slices into rings. Cut each artichoke heart into quarters. Cut tomatoes into wedges. Add prepared vegetables to potatoes in bowl and stir throughly to mix. Transfer to serving-platter and decorate with anchovy fillets, egg slices and olives. Beat olive oil with salt and pepper to taste then gradually beat in lemon juice and vinegar. Pour over salad, sprinkle with parsley and serve straight away.

STEAMED BLACKCURRANT SUET PUDDING
(Serves 4)

2 tablespoons blackcurrant jam
4 oz. plain flour (approximately ½ cup all-purpose)
¼ level teaspoon salt
1½ level teaspoons baking-powder
4 oz. fresh white breadcrumbs (approximately 3 cups)

3 oz. caster sugar (approximately ⅜ cup)
3 oz. finely shredded suet (⅜ cup)
1 large beaten egg
1 teaspoon vanilla essence
6 to 8 tablespoons cold milk to mix

Butter a 2-pint pudding basin and cover base with jam. Sift flour, salt and baking-powder into bowl. Add breadcrumbs, sugar and suet and toss ingredients lightly together. Mix to fairly soft batter with egg, vanilla and milk. Transfer to prepared basin. Cover top with double thickness of greased greaseproof paper or aluminium foil and steam steadily for 3 hours. Turn out of basin and serve with custard sauce or single cream (coffee cream).

APPLE CHARLOTTE (Serves 4)

We tend to think of all charlottes as essentially British; traditional certainly, and going far back in time to an almost forgotten age. But whether they actually originated in this country is a moot point, for the French claim they were named after Charlotte de Medici, wife of the son of the Prince of Condé, while others attribute charlottes to the wife of King George III.

1 lb. cooking apples
4 level tablespoons caster sugar
4 oz. fresh white breadcrumbs (approximately 3 cups)

1 level teaspoon finely grated lemon peel
1 level teaspoon powdered cinnamon
3 oz. melted butter

Peel, core and thinly slice apples. In a basin, combine sugar, breadcrumbs, lemon peel and cinnamon. Fill a 2-pint buttered heatproof dish with alternate layers of breadcrumb mixture and apples, beginning and ending with breadcrumbs and spooning all the melted butter both between the layers and over the top. Bake in centre of moderately hot oven (375°F. or Gas No. 5) for 45 minutes or until apples are tender and the top is a rich gold. Serve with custard sauce or cream.

Capricorn

Capricorn

THE GOAT — 21st December to 19th January

RULING PLANET — SATURN

Man is by nature a political animal.

Aristotle

Character Study — Capricornians generally are average height or shorter. They usually have long faces and necks, classical features and slim arms and legs. The nose is often prominent, the eyes tend to be blue, rounded and deep-set and the brows are well-defined. Both Capricornian men and women age well and seem to look their best in middle life. As a group they are patient, conscientious, reliable, loyal, studious, precise, neat, thrifty, strictly fair in all their judgments and honest, with a strong sense of duty towards family, friends and employers. They show shrewdness, caution and a measure of reserve in their dealings with others, and are highly efficient, business-like, diplomatic, ambitious, persistent, energetic and very self-reliant.

They are well suited to public life and many take up government appointments either as politicians, officials or judges. Others succeed in finance, agriculture, large business concerns, property and research. Both in their business and personal life, Capricornians are more fortunate in middle and old age than in youth.

Where marriage is concerned, Capricornians are in harmony with the more domesticated Cancer or Taurus or the intellectual Virgo but are out of step with Arieans and Librans.

Although they have strong constitutions (Capricornians frequently live longer than those born under any other sign), they are apt to become introspective, very depressed and despondent when inactive, and in advancing years, some develop rheumatism in the legs and other parts of the body.

Cooking — Cooking is not a natural accomplishment of Capricornians but many become first-class practical cooks through perseverance and determination. Because they are fascinated by history and so intrigued with the past, traditional dishes and ancient recipes adapted from old books appeal to them far more than anything new and up-to-the-minute, and their instinctive dislike of waste makes them very adept at turning left-overs into interesting and tasty concoctions.

Likes — Capricornians like budgeting their finances (often to the nearest penny) and adhering to a disciplined routine. They also like good quality, well-cut clothes which they know will last a long time—they are not easily swayed by trends in fashion. Green, turquoise and blue appeal to them, as do pot-plants dotted about the house, a green-house in the garden and silvery metals. They enjoy going to and giving small dinner parties and make thoughtful and able hosts and hostesses. When holidaying, Capricornians derive an inner calm from mountain and lake resorts but in their more practical moments often choose health farms and spas. They take pride and pleasure in driving well (which most of them do) and are courteous both to other road-users and pedestrians. They appreciate gifts of historical novels, biographies and autobiographies, small antique ornaments and anything practical and useful in the way of food, drinks and clothing or office accessories. Little Capricornians, as thoughtful as their elders, love interesting story-books, constructional toys and drawing and painting-books.

Dislikes — Capricornians are uneasy amid large social gatherings where most of the people are strangers, and they dislike having to make inconsequential small talk. They are embarrassed by displays of emotion, any form of extravagance and can get very irritated by untidy people about the house. The problems of domesticity hold little appeal to the career-minded Capricornian wife and mother, and although she is a most capable, efficient and fastidious housekeeper and devoted, in her reserved way, to her family, she dislikes the emotional demands made on her and sometimes has difficulty in understanding or communicating with her children, especially when they become teenagers with problems of their own.

Birth Stones—Capricornians have two birth stones; the reddish-brown velvety garnet and the striking black onyx. Garnet—which comes from the Latin 'granatus'—was a stone highly esteemed by early Crusaders, who carried it with them as a protection against battle wounds. Although garnets range in colour from purple to green, the most popular and widely worn stones are the dark red ones which come chiefly from Eastern Europe, Russia, South Africa, India, Ceylon and parts of America.

Onyx, usually jet black, is a member of the quartz family and is often used for brooches and ornamental rings.

CAPRICORN RECIPES

A FRIAR'S OMELET *c.* 1843

'Boil a dozen small cooking apples to a pulp, as for apple sauce. Stir in a quarter of a pound of butter or margarine, and the same of white sugar. When cold, add four eggs well beaten; put into a buttered baking-dish thickly strewed over with crumbs of bread, so as to stick to the bottom and sides; then put in the apple mixture; strew crumbs of bread plentifully over the top. Bake it in a very slow oven for about an hour. Send it to the table with extra sugar for sprinkling over the top. Serves about four to six.'

Adapted from *Mrs. Rundle's Domestic Cookery by a Lady*.

MINT VINEGAR

A sensible recipe from *The Practical Housewife*, published about a hundred years ago.

'This is made by putting into a wide-mouthed bottle fresh nice clean mint leaves enough to fill it loosely: then fill up the bottle with good vinegar: and after it has been stopped close for two or three weeks, it is to be poured off clean into another bottle, and kept well corked for use. Serve with lamb when mint cannot be obtained.'

Note: Wine vinegar should be used and I would also recommend sweetening the vinegar before serving. In other words, pour off as much as you need for the meal then add to it 1 or 2 teaspoons of sugar dissolved in a tablespoon of hot water.

TO PICKLE WALNUTS *c.* 1890

'A lady recommends the following receipt as very excellent for pickling walnuts . . . Gather them when dry. Take a large needle, and perforate them through in several places. Strew the bottom of a jar with best powdered ginger, crushed cloves and salt; then put in some walnuts. Then again salt, powdered ginger, crushed cloves, and so on alternately, till the jar is rather more than three-quarters full, placing plenty of salt and the spices on top. Then cover them with the best vinegar— the French vinegar is excellent. Quite fill the jar with vinegar; tie a bladder over the jar, and set by till November or December. Then pour the liquor off, and this boiled up with spices, anchovies, English shallots, and plenty of bay leaves, adding cayenne pepper, and more salt, will form a most excellent walnut catsup for fish or steaks. Then put fresh vinegar, spices, and bay-leaves, to the walnuts; fill the jar: and in a fortnight they will be fit to eat, and are very far superior to those that are soaked in salt and water, as they usually are done, besides gaining a most excellent fish sauce from the first vinegar. Those who once try this plan will never return to the old one.'

DOG'S-NOSE

A potent Victorian drink.

'Warm half a pint of ale (1¼ cups) then add a wineglassful of gin to it; then add half a pint (1¼ cups) of cold ale and serve.'

ATHOL BROSE

An old-fashioned Scottish heart-warmer.

'Add two wineglassfuls of Scotch Whisky to a wineglassful of heather-honey; mix well, and then stir in a well-beaten new-laid egg.'

VEAL, POTTED *c.* 1880

'Pound the remains of a cold fillet with mace, peppercorns, two or three cloves and a little salt, and press it well down into pots, then cover with clarified butter. Alternate layers of pounded ham and veal, or both mixed, form a fine compound for the luncheon or breakfast table.'

Note: I would mince the meat first and then season it to taste with freshly milled pepper, powdered mace and powdered cloves. I would also refrigerate the little pots.

RICHELIEU PUDDING *c.* 1885

'Steep the crumb of a large slice of bread in milk, warm as from the cow; let it rest, and then strain off the milk; beat up the yolk of an egg, mix it with the bread, also a bit of butter; put it into a saucepan, and boil till it becomes stiff; let it cool and then add some chopped parsley, thyme, pepper and salt; beat up 2 eggs; mince about one pound of any cold meat, and add all together. Boil in a basin for 3 hours, and when dished, pour a good gravy over it. I can recommend this as being good and economical.'

FRENCH WAY OF DRESSING COLD BEETROOT *c.* 1890

'Take your cold beetroot—chop it very small and put it into a saucepan to heat, with a little cream; immediately before serving, put in a spoonful of vinegar and a little brown sugar; serve hot.'

YELLOW RICE *c.* 1880

'Take one pound of rice, wash it clean, and put into a saucepan which will hold three quarts; add to it half a pound of currants picked and washed, one quarter of an ounce of the best turmeric powder, previously dissolved in a cupful of water, and a stick of cinnamon; pour over them two quarts of cold water (5 cups), place the saucepan uncovered on a moderate fire, and allow it to boil till the rice is dry, then stir in a quarter of a pound of sugar, and two ounces of butter: cover up, and place the pan near the fire for a few minutes, then mix it well and dish up. This is a favourite dish with the Javanese, and will be found excellent as a vegetable, with roast meat and poultry etc.'

Note: Use American long-grain rice for this dish.

EVERTON TOFFEE *c.* 1880

'To make this favourite and wholesome candy, take 1 lb. and a half of moist sugar, 3 oz. of butter, a teacupful and a half of water, and one lemon. Boil the sugar, butter, water, and half the rind of the lemon together, and when sufficiently done—which will be known by dropping into cold water, when it should be quite crisp—let it stand aside until the boiling has ceased, and then stir in the juice of the lemon. Butter a dish, and pour it in, about a quarter of an inch in thickness.'

A NEW METHOD OF ROASTING A GOOSE *c.* 1875

'Boil and mash some potatoes and fill the goose with them. When half roasted, take out the potatoes and have ready a stuffing of sage and parboiled onions, which put in the goose, and finish roasting. This draws out all the fat and makes it quite delicate.'

ON DRESSING NEW POTATOES *c.* 1836

'Choose the potatoes as nearly of a size as possible; wash them, and rub off the outer rind; then wipe them dry with a clean napkin. Put a quarter of a pound of fresh butter into a saucepan, set it on the fire and when it boils throw in the potatoes. Let them boil in the butter till they are done, taking care to toss them every now and then so that they may all go successfully into the boiling butter. They must be carefully watched because if done too much they shrivel up and become waxy. When the fork indicates that they are done, they must be taken out before they lose their crispness, put into a dish, and some salt sprinkled over them. As soon as they are taken from the boiling butter, a handful of parsley may be thrown into it, and, after it has had a boil or two, laid upon the potatoes as a garnish. They must be eaten immediately. This is a beautiful dish to serve up with fish, as it may be eaten alone. The butter in which the potatoes were dressed may be poured into a jar, and served again for the same purpose. Old potatoes may be cut into round pieces about the size of a large walnut, and dressed in the same way.'

HODGE PODGE

This comes from a book called *A Handbook of Cookery for School and Home*, published round about 1890 and written by a lady called Ada T. Pearson. It is a sound little book and what I especially like about it is the way the author has priced each recipe. By comparison with our present-day cost of living, it makes amusing and absorbing reading!

'Ingredients:—

2 lb. neck of mutton or shin of beef ... ... 1/2d.	1 tea-spoonful chopped parsley	}	
1 small cabbage ... ... 1d.	3 oz. pearl barley or rice	}	½d.
2 carrots }	2 tea-spoonfuls salt		
1 turnip } ... ... 1d.	½ tea-spoonful pepper		
2 onions }	2 quarts cold water		
2 pints green peas or broad beans ... ... 1½d.			
	Total		1/6d.

'Enough meat and soup for 6 persons.

Way of making: Cut the mutton in chops; wash the cabbage, cut it in pieces. Wash, peel and cut the vegetables in small pieces; wash the rice or barley. Put the meat into a sauce-pan with the cold water, bring it to the boil and skim it. Put in the barley and all the vegetables except the peas; draw the pan aside and cook slowly for 2 hours, then add the peas or beans and seasoning. Cook slowly for another half an hour and serve. Time, 3 hours.'

COLCANNON

From the same book comes this Irish recipe, which is as good a way as any of using up cold potatoes and boiled cabbage.

Ingredients:

6 or 8 cold potatoes ... ½d.	1 oz. dripping	}	
1 small boiled cabbage ... 1d.	2 tablespoonfuls milk	}	½d.
	½ tea-spoonful salt	}	
	¼ tea-spoonful pepper	}	
	Total		2d.

'Way of making: Mash the potatoes in a saucepan, chop the cabbage and beat it into the potatoes with the dripping, seasoning and milk. Beat it with a wooden spoon, while it is warming through to prevent it burning, and serve on a hot dish.'

NOTTINGHAM PUDDING *c.* 1880

A perfect apple recipe for using up garden windfalls.

'Peel six large apples, and remove the core in such a manner as to leave the fruit whole, then fill up the centre with sugar, place the fruit in a piedish and pour over a nice light batter such as used for pudding. Bake in a moderate oven for an hour.'

Note: The batter referred to in the recipe is a straightforward Yorkshire pudding one. I would recommend buttering the dish and baking in an oven temperature of 425°F. or Gas No. 7 for 30 minutes and then a temperature of 375°F. or Gas No. 5 for a further 20 to 30 minutes.

CHESHIRE PORK PIE *c.* 1880

'Take the skin off a loin of pork, and cut the loin into steaks, season with salt, pepper and dried sage. Make a good crust, line the dish with it, and put in a layer of pork, then a layer of sliced pippins [apples] dipped in sugar, then another layer of pork, and add half a pint of white wine; put some pieces of butter on the top, cover in the pie and bake in a moderate oven.'

Note: I would bake this pie at 425°F. or Gas No. 7 for 20 minutes and then at 350°F. or Gas No. 4 for approximately 1 to 1¼ hours.

HEAVENLY JAM

This jam of many fruits goes back a long, long time and the recipe was given to me with great pride by a Canadian colleague who inherited it from her mother.

4 large oranges
2 large lemons
½ pint water (1¼ cups)
12 medium pears
12 medium eating apples

12 ripe peaches or 18 ripe apricots
12 oz. granulated sugar (1½ cups) to every lb. of fruit

Wash oranges and lemons and slice thinly. Put into a large heavy preserving pan (minus pips) with the water. Bring to boil. Lower heat and boil gently for 30 minutes. Meanwhile, peel rest of fruit, remove cores and stones and chop coarsely. Add to oranges and lemons and cook a further 15 minutes. Stir in sugar and boil briskly until setting point is reached. Gently lift off scum and, as soon as jam is luke-warm, transfer to clean dry jars. Cover when completely cold.

Note: To test for setting point, pour a little jam onto a cold saucer and leave for 2 minutes in the cool. If the surface wrinkles when touched, the jam is ready. If you have a sugar (or candy) thermometer, boil jam to a temperature of 220°F.

DUCKLING BROTH (Serves 4 to 6)

A worthwhile soup for making the best possible use of a duckling carcase and set of giblets.

1 duckling carcase	3 to 4 tablespoons barley
1 set duckling giblets	1 to 2 level teaspoons salt
2 pints chicken stock (5 cups)	1 wineglass red wine
4 large carrots	handful of finely chopped
2 large onions	parsley
3 celery stalks	

Put carcase, giblets and stock into a large saucepan. Slowly bring to boil. Meanwhile, slice carrots and onions thinly. Cut celery into diagonal strips. Remove scum from soup then add prepared vegetables, barley and salt to taste. Bring to boil again, lower heat and cover pan. Simmer slowly for 2 to 2½ hours or until barley is tender. Remove bones and giblets from soup then stir in wine and parsley. Adjust seasoning to taste and serve piping hot.

Note: If liked, giblet meat can be chopped and added to soup with wine and parsley.

GOLDEN TOPPED CHICKEN PIE (Serves 4)

A tasty and nourishing dish made from left-over chicken and stale bread.

3 oz. butter or margarine
($\frac{3}{8}$ cup)

4 tablespoons grated Parmesan cheese or stale, dry cheddar

1 level teaspoon dried thyme

$\frac{1}{2}$ level teaspoon grated lemon peel

4 large slices white bread, with crusts removed

1 medium chopped onion ($\frac{1}{2}$ cup)

2 oz. sliced mushrooms (approximately $\frac{5}{8}$ cup)

3 level tablespoons flour

$\frac{1}{2}$ pint chicken stock (1$\frac{1}{4}$ cups)

8 oz. cold cooked chicken, chopped (approximately 1$\frac{1}{2}$ cups)

1 tablespoon lemon juice

3 tablespoons single cream (coffee cream)

salt and pepper to taste

Cream 1$\frac{1}{2}$ oz. butter or margarine (about 1$\frac{1}{2}$ tablespoons) with cheese, thyme and lemon peel. Spread over bread, then cut each slice into four triangles. Leave on one side. Melt remaining butter or margarine in a saucepan. Add onion and fry very gently, with lid on pan, until soft and pale gold; about 7 minutes. Add mushrooms and fry a further 5 minutes. Stir in flour, cook 2 minutes then gradually blend in stock. Cook, stirring, until mixture comes to boil and thickens. Add chicken and boil gently for 15 minutes. Stir in lemon juice and cream and season to taste with salt and pepper. Transfer to a fairly shallow ovenproof dish and arrange bread triangles attractively on top, buttered sides uppermost. Bake near top of hot oven (425°F. or Gas No. 7) for 15 to 20 minutes or until bread is crisp and golden. Serve straight away. Accompany with a crisp salad.

FLUFFY CHEESE AND PARSLEY BAKE (Serves 4)

3 large slices white bread (which can be a couple of days old)

$\frac{1}{2}$ pint milk (1$\frac{1}{4}$ cups)

4 oz. stale cheddar cheese, grated (1 cup)

1 level teaspoon made mustard

2 tablespoons chopped parsley

2 eggs, separated

salt and pepper to taste

Cut bread into cubes and put into a fairly large saucepan with the

143

milk. Stand over a low heat and whisk gently until mixture becomes smooth and thick. Beat in cheese, mustard, parsley and egg-yolks then season to taste with salt and pepper. Whip egg-whites to a stiff snow. Fold into breadcrumb mixture. Transfer to a 2½-pint buttered heatproof dish which is deep rather than shallow. Bake in centre of a moderately hot oven (375°F. or Gas No. 5) for 35 to 40 minutes, or until well puffed and golden. Serve straight away with baked tomatoes.

Aquarius

Aquarius

THE WATER BEARER — 20th January to 18th February

RULING PLANETS — SATURN AND URANUS

*Two things fill the mind with ever-increasing wonder and awe,
the more often and the more intensely the mind of thought is drawn
to them; the starry heavens above me and the moral law within me.*
Immanuel Kant — *Critique of Practical Reason*

Character Study — Aquarians are handsome and distinguished-looking people with widely spaced and deep-set eyes—often grey or blue—which are both beautiful and compelling. They are average to tall in height with large heads, high intellectual foreheads and good profiles. They have clear complexions, fine skins and soft, silky hair and they are sturdily built, inclining towards stoutness in middle age. As a group, Aquarians have sound reasoning powers and intellectual and practical capabilities and are both philosophical and instinctively humane, with a profound concern over man's inhumanity to man. Freedom is placed high on the list of priorities by Aquarians and they will not be restricted in mind or deed by the opinions of other people or accepted standards of convention. They must, and will, go their own way, irrespective of any adverse criticism levelled at them for it. Generally speaking, most people born under this sign are idealistic, honest, sincere, self-controlled, patient, studious, analytical, helpful towards others, outspoken and candid (too much sometimes), intuitive, sensitive, and lovers of nature, music and literature. They are also independent, original, inventive and ingenious, with marked organizing ability. Some tend to be penny wise and pound foolish and are over-generous to humanitarian charities, forgetting that their own immediate family may be an equally worthy cause!

Because of their characteristics, many Aquarians are enigmatic and a bit difficult to live with and must therefore choose a partner with more care, perhaps, than many of the other signs. They are happiest with Librans and Geminians but tend to be out of harmony with Taureans, Leonians and Scorpionians.

As a result of their high intelligence and intellect, most Aquarians have distinctive careers, choosing responsible positions in public life, all branches of science (including medicine and sociology), research, literature, music and fashion design.

Those Aquarians who sit at their work should, in their spare time, get as much exercise as possible in the fresh air to prevent the onset of circulatory disorders, to which they are prone. They should also take care of their eyes as their sight is inclined to deteriorate early in life. Apart from this they are healthy, robust people with an enormous amount of resilience.

Cooking — Many Aquarians are competent cooks, always eager to try new and unusual recipe ideas. They are enthusiastic gadget collectors and users and enjoy making up dishes in conjunction with blenders, mixers and pressure cookers. The humane streak in some Aquarians compels them to follow a vegetarian diet and forgo all flesh foods.

Likes — Aquarians like to dress casually, and often unconventionally, and are not too concerned over lack of co-ordination in their wardrobes. All shades of green and blue please them, as do growing vegetables and herbs, buying antiques, going to the theatre, ballet, opera and concerts, driving a mechanically sound car (no matter what it looks like), following the rule of the road and having long and deep discussions on controversial subjects. They derive deep satisfaction from adventurous and educational holidays, and nothing delights them more than a few weeks spent in exploring an historical town with ancient buildings, monuments and museums. Most Aquarians welcome gifts of rare and interesting books (the rarer the better), old porcelain, cut glass and figurines. Little Aquarians like jigsaw puzzles, historical story-books and all sorts of indoor games which stretch the imagination.

Dislikes — Aquarians dislike unimportant party chatter, taking advice, going to large parties purely to socialize, being too wrapped up in home and family affairs, bright and unsubtle colours, ostentatious people and things, shopping in large, busy and crowded stores, excess formality in their personal lives and over-possessive partners and children.

Birth Stone — The Aquarian's stone is the vibrant mauve amethyst, which is a member of the quartz family. Amethysts, which come mainly from Russia, Ceylon and South America, were believed by the ancient Greeks to protect a man from his own follies and in particular against drunkenness. They are still considered to be protective and beneficial to those who wear them.

AQUARIUS RECIPES

TOMATO SHERRY SOUP (Serves 6)

A brand new idea in chilled soups.

1 can (10½ oz.) condensed tomato soup
3 to 4 dessertspoons dry sherry
¼ pint double cream (⅔ cup whipping cream)
1 teaspoon Worcestershire sauce
snipped chives or chopped parsley

Put soup into a bowl. Add 1 soup can very hot water (just off the boil). Whisk until completely smooth then whisk in sherry, cream and Worcestershire sauce. Chill 3 to 4 hours. Just before serving, stir well, ladle into soup bowls and sprinkle chives or parsley over the top of each.

BLENDER VICHYSSOISE (Serves 6)

A cool classic summer soup, quickly made in a blender.

2 large leeks
1 large onion
1 lb. potatoes
2 oz. butter (¼ cup)
¾ pint chicken stock (2 cups)
¾ pint milk (2 cups)
salt and white pepper to taste
½ pint double cream (1¼ cups whipping cream)
2 to 3 level tablespoons snipped chives

Slit leeks lengthwise and wash thoroughly under cold running water. Finely chop white part of leek only. Peel onion and chop. Peel and wash potatoes and cut into quarters. Melt butter in saucepan. Add leek and onion and fry gently, in covered saucepan, until soft but not brown;

about 7 minutes. Add potatoes, stock, milk and salt and pepper to taste. Cook gently until potatoes are just tender. Put half the soup into the blender. Cover and blend until smooth. Pour into large serving-bowl. Repeat with rest of soup and pour into bowl. Stir in unwhipped cream, scatter chives over the top and refrigerate for a minimum of 4 hours. Serve in soup bowls or cups.

CURRIED CELERY SOUP (Serves 4)

An interesting soup for all vegetarians.

1 garlic clove (optional)	2 level teaspoons curry powder
1 can (10½ oz.) condensed cream of celery soup	1 tablespoon lemon juice pinch of cayenne pepper
1 soup can single cream (coffee cream)	about 4 teaspoons toasted coconut

Rub inside of saucepan to be used for soup with cut clove of garlic. Add can of soup, cream, curry powder, lemon juice and cayenne pepper. Bring just up to the boil, whisking gently all the time. Ladle into 4 warm soup bowls and sprinkle the tops of each with toasted coconut. Serve hot.

APRICOT MILK SHAKE (Serves 4)

Put 4 heaped tablespoons apricot jam into blender. Add 1 pint (2½ cups) chilled milk and 4 heaped tablespoons vanilla ice-cream. Blend until smooth and frothy. Pour into 4 glasses and serve straight away.

BLENDER AVOCADO MAYONNAISE

1 large avocado	¼ teaspoon paprika
4 tablespoons salad oil	½ teaspoon mustard
1 egg	½ teaspoon Worcestershire sauce
juice of 1 medium lemon	½ teaspoon salt
¼ teaspoon sugar	

Peel avocado and cut flesh into small pieces. Put into blender with remaining ingredients. Blend 10 to 20 seconds or until smooth and creamy. Adjust seasoning to taste and thin down with a little cream if mayonnaise is too thick for your needs. Keep covered in the refrigerator up to 3 days. Delicious in salads over eggs, poultry and vegetables. Sufficient for about 4 servings.

149

SPEEDY APPLE SAUCE (Serves 6)

An apple sauce for lamb and pork made literally in seconds in a blender.

4 medium cooking apples
4 tablespoons water
2 tablespoons lemon juice

pinch EACH, powdered cinnamon and cloves
2 tablespoons granulated sugar
4 drops red food colouring

Peel and core apples and cut into cubes. Put into blender with all the other ingredients. Blend until smooth and serve straight away. If not required for immediate use, tip sauce into saucepan and bring just up to boil. This will prevent discolouration.

MARROW À L'ESPAGNOLE (Serves 4)

3 large skinned tomatoes
1 large onion
1 oz. butter (⅛ cup)
2 teaspoons salad oil
1 medium sized marrow

salt and pepper to taste
½ level teaspoon dried basil or mixed herbs
3 tablespoons water

Slice tomatoes and onion. Heat butter and oil in a large saucepan. Add tomatoes and onion and fry gently, with lid on pan, until onions are soft; about 15 minutes. Meanwhile, peel marrow and slice. Remove centre seeds and cut marrow rings into moderate sized chunks. Add to pan. Season to taste with salt and pepper then add remaining 2 ingredients. Simmer very gently until marrow is just tender. Serve with all egg and cheese dishes.

RICE-AND-MUSHROOM-STUFFED PEPPERS
(Serves 4)

4 medium sized green peppers
2 oz. butter or margarine (¼ cup)
1 medium finely chopped onion (½ cup)
¼ lb. raw long-grain rice (½ cup uncooked)
½ pint water (1¼ cups)

4 oz. sliced mushrooms (1¼ cups)
2 medium skinned and chopped tomatoes
1 level teaspoon salt
¼ level teaspoon dried basil pepper to taste
¼ pint (⅔ cup) tomato juice

Cut tops off peppers and remove inside fibres and seeds. Wash thoroughly and put into large saucepan. Cover with water and bring to boil. Remove from heat immediately and pour off water. Stand peppers upside down to drain on paper towels. Heat butter or margarine in saucepan. Add onion and fry very gently, with lid on pan, for about 10 minutes or until onions are soft and just beginning to colour. Add rice and fry a further 2 minutes, stirring. Pour in water then add mushrooms, tomatoes, salt, basil and pepper to taste. Cover pan and cook gently until rice grains are plump and fluffy and have absorbed all the moisture; about 20 minutes. Spoon into peppers and stand in baking dish. Spoon tomato juice over peppers into dish. Cook in centre of moderately hot oven (375°F. or Gas No. 5) for 30 minutes, basting at least twice with juice during cooking. Serve hot.

CHEESE AND WALNUT SOUFFLÉ (Serves 4)

2 oz. butter or margarine ($\frac{1}{4}$ cup)	2 oz. finely ground walnuts (approximately $\frac{1}{4}$ cup)
4 level tablespoons flour	salt, pepper and mustard to
$\frac{1}{2}$ pint milk ($1\frac{1}{4}$ cups)	taste
6 oz. grated cheddar cheese (2 cups)	5 medium sized eggs, separated

Brush a straight-sided soufflé dish measuring $7\frac{1}{2}$ inches in diameter with butter. Melt butter or margarine in a large saucepan. Stir in flour and cook gently for 2 minutes without browning. Gradually blend in milk. Cook, whisking continuously, until sauce comes to boil and thickens sufficiently to leave sides of saucepan clean; about 4 minutes. Remove from heat and beat in cheese, walnuts, salt, pepper, and mustard to taste and egg-yolks. Beat egg-whites to a stiff and peaky snow. Gently fold into cheese mixture with a large metal spoon. Pour into prepared dish and bake in the centre of a moderately hot oven (375°F. or Gas No. 5) for 45 minutes or until soufflé is well-risen—with a high, tall crown—and golden brown. Serve immediately (because the soufflé falls quickly) with a mixed salad tossed with French dressing.

Note: Please do not open the oven door while the soufflé is cooking or it will sink in the middle.

HOT ARTICHOKES WITH BLENDER
HOLLANDAISE SAUCE (Serves 4 as an *hors-d'œuvre*)

4 medium globe artichokes
water
salt

1 tablespoon wine vinegar
1 tablespoon salad oil

Sauce

6 oz. melted butter ($\frac{2}{3}$ cup)
3 egg-yolks
1 tablespoon lemon juice
1 tablespoon wine vinegar
pinch of sugar

$\frac{1}{2}$ level teaspoon prepared
mustard
$\frac{1}{4}$ level teaspoon salt
$\frac{1}{8}$ teaspoon pepper

Wash artichokes by plunging heads in and out of a bowl of cold water. Cut off stems then snip away tops of leaves with sharp kitchen scissors. Place upright in a large saucepan (stem ends standing on base of pan) then half-fill with water. Add about 1 teaspoon salt, vinegar and salad oil. Bring slowly to boil, lower heat and cover. Simmer 45 minutes. Lift out of pan and drain thoroughly. At this point make the Hollandaise sauce. Put butter into saucepan and leave it over a very low heat until it is hot and just beginning to sizzle. Put egg-yolks into blender. Bring lemon juice and vinegar just up to the boil. Add to yolks with sugar, mustard, salt and pepper. Cover and blend 10 seconds. Uncover and with blender set at high speed, add butter in slow steady stream. Blend about 45 seconds, when sauce should be thick and smooth. Serve straight away with the still warm artichokes.

BENEDICT EGGS

Another dish which can be made successfully with the Blender Hollandaise Sauce given above. Serve it either as an *hors-d'œuvre*, light luncheon or late supper snack. Split 2 large soft rolls (such as baps) and toast until golden. Top each with 2 grilled bacon rashers (bacon strips) and a lightly poached egg. Coat completely with Hollandaise sauce and dust with the merest hint of cayenne pepper. For lunch or supper accompany with small individual salads.

HEALTH FOOD SALAD (Serves 4)

6 oz. shell-shaped pasta
(3 cups cooked)
1 small green pepper
1 small onion
2 dozen stoned olives
4 oz. cheddar cheese

4 hard-boiled eggs
4 skinned tomatoes, chopped
about ¼ pint French dressing
(⅔ cup)
lettuce leaves

Cook pasta in boiling salted water as directed on the packet. Drain, cool and put into mixing-bowl. Halve green pepper, remove fibres and seeds and chop flesh finely. Coarsely grate onion. Slice olives thinly. Cut cheese into tiny cubes. Chop eggs. Cut tomatoes into wedges. Put all prepared ingredients into bowl with pasta and toss with sufficient French dressing to moisten, adding if necessary a little more or less than the amount given in the list of ingredients. Line 4 individual plates or bowls with lettuce and top with equal amounts of salad. Serve with brown bread and butter.

STUFFED LOIN OF PORK WITH APPLE GLAZE
(Serves 4 to 5)

2 to 3 lb. loin of pork

Glaze

1½ lb. cooking apples
3 tablespoons water
4 oz. brown sugar (¾ cup)
2 tablespoons Worcestershire
sauce

½ level teaspoon mustard
2 cloves
2 teaspoons cornflour (corn
starch)

Stuffing

2 tablespoons butter
1 small chopped onion
(approximately ¼ cup)
2 oz. boiled long-grain rice,
weighed before cooking
(1 cup cooked rice)

½ apple (taken from above),
peeled and chopped finely
grated peel and juice of 1
medium lemon
1 tablespoon chopped parsley
2 level teaspoons dried thyme
salt and pepper

Make a slit in the joint between bone and thick piece of meat, but do not cut to end of bone. Reserve ½ an apple for stuffing. To make glaze, peel, core and slice remaining apples thinly. Put into saucepan with 1 tablespoon water. Cook, in covered pan, until soft and pulpy. Stir in sugar, Worcestershire sauce, mustard and cloves. Cook gently for 2 minutes. Remove cloves then *purée* apples in blender or liquidizer (or rub through fine sieve).

Meanwhile, prepare stuffing. Heat butter in a pan, add onion and fry gently until soft and pale gold. Stir in rice, chopped apple, lemon peel and juice, parsley and thyme. Season to taste with salt and pepper then bind together with about 2 tablespoons of apple glaze.

Place stuffing between bone and meat and tie joint with string. Stand on a rack in a roasting tin, cover with apple glaze and cook in centre of hot oven (425°F. or Gas No. 7) for 1½ hours. Baste once more with apple glaze during roasting. Transfer pork to a platter and keep hot. Pour off fat from roasting tin and stir in cornflour (corn starch), mixed to a smooth cream with 2 tablespoons water. Add remaining apple glaze. Slowly bring to boil, stirring. Cook 1 minute then pour into sauce boat. Serve with the pork.

SPICED BEEF (Serves 4 to 6 people about twice)

This is the beef one finds in salt beef bars, nestling, still hot and spread with mustard, between very fresh slices of white or rye bread and accompanied invariably with sweet-sour pickled cucumbers. As a thick, juicy sandwich it makes a feast of a snack but it is just as good served hot with French fried potatoes or cold with salad and pickles. It makes sense to buy a fairly large piece of brisket, about 4 to 5 lb., so that you have enough meat for one hot meal, one cold meal and still some left over for sandwiches. It goes further than a roast and is one of the less expensive cuts of beef.

4 to 5 lb. piece of rolled and salted brisket	1 heaped tablespoon pickling spice
3 large onions	2 bay leaves
2 large carrots	

Soak meat overnight in cold water. Drain and put into pressure cooker. (If it is too much to fit into the cooker, cut in half and cook both pieces together.) Cover with cold water. Bring to boil and drain. Half fill the pan with fresh water. Add whole peeled onions and carrots, the pickling spice and bay leaves. Cook at 15 lb. pressure for 1 hour. Leave to cool off slightly before slicing. Left over brisket should be foil-wrapped and refrigerated.

POULET AU RIZ (Serves 6 to 8)

A mild and delicate chicken dish which is best made with a boiling fowl.

1 boiling fowl, about 4 to 5 lb.	3 level tablespoons flour
2 large onions	2 tablespoons lemon juice
2 large carrots	seasoning to taste
2 celery stalks	2 egg-yolks
handful of parsley	4 tablespoons single cream
1 small bay leaf	(coffee cream)
2 level teaspoons salt	12 oz. long-grain rice
1½ oz. butter (about 1½	(approximately 1½ cups)
tablespoons)	

Put fowl into pressure cooker. Two-thirds fill pan with water and bring to boil. Remove scum then add onions and carrots, broken celery stalks, parsley, bay leaf and salt. Cook at 15 lb. pressure for 30 minutes. Uncover and ladle ¾ pint (approximately 2 cups) chicken stock into measuring jug. Leave chicken in pressure cooker and stand over low heat to keep hot. Melt butter in saucepan. Stir in flour and cook 2 minutes without browning. Gradually blend in ¾ pint chicken stock. Cook, stirring, until sauce comes to boil and thickens. Add lemon juice, season to taste and simmer 5 minutes. Meanwhile, carve chicken into slices and joints. Arrange on a warm serving-dish. Beat egg-yolks and cream well together and stir into hot sauce. Pour at once over chicken and serve straight away with freshly boiled rice, into which ½ to 1 table-spoon butter has been stirred.

CHICKEN PURÉE SOUP (Serves about 4)

A natural follow-up of the above recipe.

Put remaining chicken stock from pressure cooker into blender, with the onions, carrots, and celery. Blend until smooth. Pour into saucepan and slowly bring to boil. Remove from heat and add 2 tablespoons white wine, sherry or lemon juice and 3 tablespoons evaporated milk or single cream (coffee cream). Re-heat without boiling. Ladle into warm soup bowls and sprinkle the top of each lightly with curry powder or paprika.

LINZERTORTE (Serves about 6 to 8)

A Continental speciality cake.

3 oz. whole almonds, unblanched ($\frac{1}{2}$ cup)
4 oz. plain flour (approximately $\frac{1}{2}$ cup all-purpose)
1 level teaspoon cinnamon
3 oz. butter ($\frac{3}{8}$ cup)

3 oz. caster sugar (approximately $\frac{3}{8}$ cup)
1 egg-yolk
raspberry jam
1 egg-white
sifted icing sugar (confectioner's sugar)

Grind almonds, with their skins, in a blender, electric grinder or coffee mill. Sift flour and cinnamon into bowl. Rub in butter. Add nuts and sugar, and mix to a stiff and pliable dough with some of the egg-yolk. Wrap in foil and refrigerate for 1 hour. Roll out three-quarters of the pastry fairly *thickly* and use to line a 7-inch flan ring standing on a lightly buttered baking tray. Fill with raspberry jam. Roll out rest of pastry fairly thinly and cut into narrow strips. Arrange in a trellis design over top of Linzertorte, making sure strips are well pressed into edges. Brush it with lightly beaten egg-white then bake in centre of moderate oven (350°F. or Gas No. 4) for 45 minutes. Remove flan ring when Linzertorte is lukewarm then dust top thickly with icing, or confectioner's, sugar. Cut into wedges when cold.

SUMMER FRUIT FOOL (Serves 4)

$\frac{1}{2}$ lb. strawberries
2 large bananas
$\frac{1}{2}$ level teaspoon finely grated orange peel

2 to 3 tablespoons granulated sugar
$\frac{1}{4}$ pint double cream ($\frac{2}{3}$ cup whipping cream)

Wash strawberries and reserve 4 for decoration. Put remainder into blender with peeled banana chunks, orange peel and sugar. Cover and blend until smooth. Beat cream until thick. Gently fold in strawberry mixture. Transfer to 4 sundae glasses and refrigerate for about 1 hour. Decorate each with 1 sliced strawberry before serving.

HAZELNUT ICE-CREAM (Serves 8 to 10)

¾ pint undiluted evaporated
milk (approximately 2 cups)
6 oz. caster sugar
(approximately ¾ cup)
2 teaspoons vanilla essence

½ pint double cream (1¼ cups
whipping cream)
5 level tablespoons finely ground
hazelnuts

Set refrigerator control to lowest setting. Wash and dry 2 ice-cube trays. Pour evaporated milk into a saucepan. Add sugar and vanilla and leave over a low heat, stirring, until sugar dissolves. Cool. Pour into prepared trays and put into freezing compartment of refrigerator. Leave until mixture has frozen about ½ inch round sides of trays. Spoon into chilled bowl and break up with a fork. Beat with electric or rotary beater until completely smooth. Whip cream until thick. Fold into ice-cream mixture with hazelnuts. When mixture is smooth and well blended return to trays and cover each with foil. Freeze until firm; a minimum of 2 hours.

STRAWBERRY GÂTEAU (Serves 8)

3 oz. plain flour
(approximately ⅜ cup all-
purpose flour)
pinch of salt

3 oz. caster sugar (3 level
tablespoons)
3 large eggs

Butter Cream Filling

4 oz. softened butter (½ cup)
8 oz. sifted icing sugar
(approximately 2 cups
confectioner's sugar)

1 tablespoon Kirsch, Cointreau
or Grand Marnier

Decoration

8 oz. fresh strawberries

3 dessertspoons red-currant jelly

Brush base and sides of two 7-inch sandwich tins with melted butter. Line bases with greaseproof paper and brush with more butter. Sift flour and salt twice onto a sheet of greaseproof paper. Put sugar and eggs into bowl of mixer. Whisk at high speed for approximately 3 minutes or until mixture is very thick, pale in colour and at least twice its original volume. Sprinkle flour on top and gently cut and fold into egg mixture with a large metal spoon. Transfer to prepared sandwich tins and bake in centre of moderate oven (350°F. or Gas No. 4) for 15 to 20 minutes or until cakes are well risen and golden. Leave in tin 5 minutes then turn out onto a sheet of paper, which is standing on a damp tea-towel. Dust the paper with a little sifted icing or confectioner's sugar first.

To make butter cream, put softened butter into bowl of mixer. Beat 2 minutes then gradually beat in sifted icing (or confectioner's) sugar. Continue beating for 3 to 4 minutes or until the mixture is light and fluffy. Gradually add liqueur and beat a further minute. Sandwich cold cakes together with half the cream. Spread remainder over top of cake then cover with halved strawberries. Melt red-currant jelly in saucepan over low heat and brush over strawberries. Chill about 30 minutes before serving.

Pisces

Pisces

THE FISHES — 19th February to 20th March

RULING PLANETS — JUPITER AND NEPTUNE

This world is a comedy to those that think, a tragedy to those that feel.

Horace Walpole

Character Study — Pisceans vary in looks according to when they were born. Those with birthdays in February and the early part of March are often below average height with thick limbs and small dimpled hands and feet. They tend towards plumpness and the women of this sign are sometimes broad-hipped, giving them a pear-shaped appearance. Many Pisceans have fair skins and pale complexions and nearly all have large, expressive eyes which are light in colour and attractively shaped. The head and face are large in proportion to the body and the hair is thick and plentiful. As the birthday approaches the middle of March, Pisceans are notably taller, with longer limbs and larger hands and feet. Their heads and faces are in better proportion and they can look slim, graceful and athletic. The majority of Pisceans are highly emotional, highly charged people with uncanny powers of intuition; they have a unique talent—a gift if you like—of knowing about what *will* happen before it does, and their sudden premonitions, though scorned by some, are usually marked by surprising accuracy. They are extremely sensitive to atmosphere and will retreat into an icy shell if they feel they are surrounded by unsympathetic people. They lack confidence and therefore must always be with those who understand and appreciate their changing moods and who will give them encouragement, praise and incentive to reach the heights of which they are capable. Pisceans are tremendously versatile people who, because

160

of their dual sign (two fish swimming in opposite directions) are able to undertake two projects at once and succeed at both. They are characterized by weakness and strength, by their tolerance and intolerance, by their practical and artistic qualities and by their hospitality to all. They are loyal, shy, highly imaginative, charming, tactful, warm-hearted and kind, romantic, generous to those they like and the opposite to those they don't, keen and responsive students, vague, indecisive, impatient, impulsive, inclined to be disorganized and untidy and ever sympathetic to anyone in trouble and need, the young and the old, all dumb creatures and lame dogs. They cannot endure the suffering of others and are always striving to go to the aid of humanity. They are patient, impressionable and long-suffering and capable of extreme happiness and gaiety (with a good sense of fun) and extreme gloom and sadness depending on environment, circumstances and companions.

Most Pisceans worry and it is this inherent anxiety which produces nervous and functional illnesses. They are not particularly strong constitutionally either and are subject to infections, blood disorders and varicose veins. They also suffer with their feet and for this reason should always buy good quality, well-fitting shoes and pay regular visits to chiropodists.

Those born under the sign of Pisces have, because of their versatility, a wide choice of careers open to them, including nursing, medicine, journalism, archaeology, novel writing, mathematics, banking and accountancy. Others go in for travel (and become stewards and stewardesses on ships and aircraft), music, painting, sculpture, poetry writing, advertising, public relations, home economics, charitable work, religion, interior and fashion design, script-writing, acting, large-scale catering and hotel management.

Early marriage can be disastrous for Pisceans in that they fall in love with love rather than their partners and then, after it is too late, wonder why they got involved in the first place! Later marriages stand a far greater chance of success, especially if they choose a Cancer or Scorpio partner. By some curious twist of fate, Pisceans and Virgonians—direct opposites—are often drawn to each other and although there are major differences in their attitudes to life and situations, they seem to have an intuitive understanding of each other's problems. The temperamental Piscean inspires and stimulates the Virgo, while the well-controlled Virgo keeps the Piscean on a more rational and balanced plane.

Cooking — All Pisceans love to eat. They are inspired and creative cooks and have a talent for giving the very simplest of meals a touch of artistry. All unusual, exotic, foreign and rich foods appeal strongly to this group and because they have a good eye for colour, anything they serve will be colourfully and tastefully garnished. Perhaps it is because they are one of the water signs that many Pisceans enjoy cooking and eating fish foods of all descriptions.

Likes — Pisceans—even in old age—enjoy the company of young people. They are at their happiest in loose, casual and well-cut clothes but spasmodically follow trends in fashion to the letter, dressing more daringly, perhaps, than many other people would think of doing. They find light, gentle colours soothing and indeed look their best in pale lemons, pinks, greens, blues and greys. All Pisceans are attracted to travel, the sea, lakes, rivers and water sports and adore lazy holidays on sun-soaked romantic beaches and the luxury of first-class hotels and cruise ships. They adapt well to new surroundings and love shopping in foreign cities, wandering through markets and absorbing all the local colour. They enjoy collecting genuine paintings and antiques if they have enough money, or bric-à-brac if they haven't, restful interior *décor* featuring all tones of green, blue, pink or purple relieved with white, house-plants, herb borders, attending dinner parties at the homes of people they know and like, giving dinner and cocktail parties, stimulating conversation, going to the theatre, night-clubs and expensive restaurants, being devoted parents and receiving gifts of jewellery, antiques, luxury toiletries, unusual and exotic foods, accessories such as scarves, ties and handkerchiefs and gift tokens for records and books. Little Pisceans enjoy puzzles, magic, chemistry and cooking-sets, painting-kits, pretty dolls and clothes (for girls) and tool kits (for boys).

Dislikes — All Pisceans dislike having to suffer fools gladly, routine, budgeting and dieting for any length of time; they start off enthusiastically and then lose interest halfway through. Making decisions worries them and consequently when they go shopping they either buy impulsively or are persuaded into buying something totally unsuitable by over-zealous sales staff. They are irritated by pettiness, meanness and narrowness of outlook in others, racial and religious prejudice, badly served food in restaurants and being reminded about their own vagueness.

Birth Stones — Pisceans have two birth stones from which to choose; the blue-green aquamarine and the less attractive bloodstone or heliotrope. Aquamarines, a member of the beryl family, are said to be the seafarer's gem, protecting those who travel over water from misfortune and bad luck. They come from Russia, South America and parts of Africa, and in olden times beryls were used by the Germans to make spectacles—hence their name of '*Brille*' for eye-glasses.

Bloodstones are usually dark green stones flecked with red, and are found in parts of America, Europe, Rusia, Canada and India.

PISCES RECIPES

BORSHCH—RUSSIAN BEETROOT SOUP
(Serves 6)

1 large carrot
1 large onion
1 small turnip
1 small parsnip
2 medium sized beets
2 celery stalks
½ lb. finely shredded white cabbage (about 3 cups)
2 tablespoons chopped parsley

2 skinned and chopped tomatoes
2 tablespoons tomato paste
2½ pints beef stock (6 cups)
1 bay leaf
juice of ½ large lemon
2 teaspoons sugar
salt and pepper to taste
¼ pint soured cream (⅔ cup dairy soured cream)

Peel first 5 ingredients. Grate fairly coarsely. Cut celery into thin strips. Put into large saucepan with cabbage, parsley, tomatoes, tomato paste, beef stock and bay leaf. Bring to boil, stirring. Cover pan and lower heat. Simmer 45 minutes. Add lemon juice, sugar and salt and pepper to taste. Continue simmering until vegetables are tender; about 30 minutes. Remove bay leaf. Ladle Borshch into warm soup bowls. Add about 1 tablespoon soured cream to each serving.

HOT STRAWBERRY SOUP (Serves 6)

For those June and July days that do not flame quite as much as they should!

1½ lb. strawberries
1½ pints cold water (4 cups)
1½ large slices white bread, cubed
6 tablespoons sugar
1 wineglass white wine

2 level teaspoons cornflour (corn starch)
1 tablespoon cold water
red food colouring
¼ pint single cream (⅔ cup coffee cream)

Wash and halve strawberries. Put into saucepan with water and bread cubes. Bring to boil, stirring, and lower heat. Cover pan and simmer gently for 30 minutes. Rub through a sieve (or liquidize in blender) then return to clean saucepan. Add sugar, wine and the cornflour, mixed to a smooth cream with water. Bring to boil, stirring, and simmer 3 minutes. Colour deep pink with food colouring then pour into 6 warm bowls. Add equal amounts of cream to each then quickly stir round with the spoon to get a rippled effect. Serve straight away.

SALMON-STUFFED MUSHROOMS (Serves 6 as an *hors-d'œuvre*)

18 large flat mushrooms, peeled
1 can (about 8 oz.) red salmon
1½ oz. fresh white breadcrumbs (about ¾ cup)
1 small grated onion

½ level teaspoon finely grated lemon peel
1 beaten egg
3 to 4 tablespoons French dressing

Remove stalks from mushrooms and reserve. Stand mushrooms in large buttered roasting tin. Chop stalks finely. Flake salmon with 2 forks. Stir in mushroom stalks, breadcrumbs, onion and lemon peel. Bind with beaten egg and French dressing. Pile equal amounts on top of mushrooms and bake near top of moderately hot oven (375°F. or Gas No. 5) for 15 minutes. Serve hot, allowing 3 per person.

FISH PLAKI (Serves 4)

4 thick cod or haddock steaks (each 4 to 6 oz.)
salt and pepper

3 tomatoes, peeled and quartered
2 tablespoons chopped parsley

1 tablespoon lemon juice
¼ pint olive oil (⅔ cup)
2 large onions, thinly sliced
1 garlic clove, finely chopped

1 tablespoon Worcestershire
sauce
¼ pint warm water (⅔ cup)
1 lemon, sliced

Sprinkle fish with salt, pepper and lemon juice. Heat oil in large frying-pan or skillet. Add onion slices and garlic and fry until lightly brown. Add tomatoes, parsley, Worcestershire sauce and water and simmer, uncovered, for 10 minutes. Add fish, standing a slice of lemon on top of each steak. Cover and poach very gently for 30 minutes. Either serve directly from the pan or skillet or spoon onion and tomato mixture onto a warm platter and arrange steaks on top. Serve with either fluffy rice or potatoes and accompany with a lettuce and cucumber salad.

CURRIED CRUMBLE FISH-PIE (Serves 4)

Curry powder and paprika add an unusual piquancy to this simple fish-pie.

1 lb. cod or haddock fillet
1 large onion, quartered
1 bay leaf
2 cloves
1 teaspoon salt
shake of pepper

¼ pint water (⅔ cup)
¼ pint milk (⅔ cup)
3 level tablespoons cornflour
(corn starch)
3 extra tablespoons cold water
seasoning to taste

Curry Crumble Topping

4 oz. plain flour (approximately
½ cup all-purpose)
½ level teaspoon salt

2 level teaspoons curry powder
1 level teaspoon paprika
2 oz. butter (¼ cup)

Skin fish. Put into shallow pan with all remaining ingredients except cornflour, extra water and seasoning to taste. Slowly bring to boil. Cover and poach gently for 15 minutes. Strain liquor and reserve ½ pint (1¼ cups). Flake fish with 2 forks. Mix cornflour to smooth cream with extra water. Combine with fish liquor and pour into saucepan. Cook, stirring, until sauce comes to boil and thickens. Adjust seasoning to taste. Add fish and transfer mixture to buttered heatproof dish, about 1½-pint size. To make crumble, sift dry ingredients into bowl. Rub in butter finely then sprinkle thickly over fish mixture. Cook in centre of moderately hot oven (400°F. or Gas No. 6) for about 20 minutes or until crumble is pale straw colour. Serve straight away.

HASHED HADDOCK (Serves 4)

1 lb. cooked haddock fillet
2 oz. butter (¼ cup)
2 level tablespoons flour
½ pint milk (1¼ cups)

2 hard-boiled eggs, chopped
salt and pepper to taste
1 lb. freshly boiled potatoes
2 extra tablespoons cold milk
1 tablespoon chopped parsley

Flake fish with 2 forks, discarding skin and bones if any. Melt half the butter in a saucepan. Stir in flour and cook gently for 2 minutes without browning. Gradually blend in milk. Cook, stirring, until sauce comes to the boil and thickens. Simmer 3 minutes then stir in chopped eggs, the flaked fish and plenty of salt and pepper to taste. Cover and leave over a very low heat. Mash potatoes finely then beat to a cream with rest of butter and milk. Arrange in a ring on a warm platter then fill centre with fish mixture. Sprinkle with parsley and serve straight away.

CRAB LOUIS (Serves 6)

A light luncheon or supper dish.

½ pint thick mayonnaise
  (1¼ cups)
2 to 3 tablespoons chilli sauce
1 tablespoon lemon juice
4 tablespoons soured cream
  (dairy soured cream)
½ small green pepper, very
  finely chopped

2 tablespoons chopped spring
  onions (with some green
  parts included)
lettuce leaves
1 lb. canned or fresh crabmeat
  (approximately 2 cups)
2 hard-boiled eggs
2 skinned tomatoes

Combine mayonnaise with chilli sauce, lemon juice, soured cream, green pepper and spring onions. Line a platter with lettuce leaves and arrange crabmeat on top. Coat with mayonnaise mixture then garnish with slices of egg and tomato.

Note: Due to the addition of chilli sauce, this dish is inclined to be on the hot side. For a milder version, reduce the chilli sauce to taste.

CALVES' LIVER CHARMAINE (Serves 4)

4 slices calves' liver, each about
4 oz.
2 level tablespoons flour,
well-seasoned with salt and
pepper
1 oz. butter ($\frac{1}{8}$ cup)
2 teaspoons salad oil
1 medium chopped onion
($\frac{1}{2}$ cup)

2 tablespoons dry sherry
3 tablespoons water
3 tablespoons mayonnaise or
salad cream
3 tablespoons soured cream
(dairy soured cream)
paprika

Coat liver in seasoned flour. Heat butter and oil in frying-pan or skillet. Add onion and fry gently, with lid on pan, until very pale gold and soft. Add liver (and any loose flour) and fry briskly until lightly brown. Add sherry and water and simmer gently 10 minutes. Transfer liver to warm platter. Stir mayonnaise and soured cream into pan juices and re-heat without boiling. Pour over liver and sprinkle lightly with paprika. Serve with creamy mashed potatoes and freshly boiled carrots tossed in butter.

BRAINS WITH BLACK BUTTER SAUCE AND CAPERS (Serves 4)

One is always hesitant about suggesting brains (except to the 'try anything once' Piscean!), yet they are mild and delicate in flavour, very pleasant to eat and remarkably popular in expensive restaurants, where they are dished up with great aplomb and almost courtly reverence!

4 sheep's brains
cold water
2 tablespoons lemon juice
lukewarm water
2 peppercorns
$\frac{1}{2}$ small bay leaf

sprig of parsley
1 teaspoon salt
3 oz. unsalted butter
1 teaspoon wine vinegar
3 level dessertspoons capers

Put brains into bowl. Cover with cold water and lemon juice. Soak for 3 hours. Drain, return to bowl and cover with lukewarm water. Soak 15 minutes, drain and remove all traces of blood, skin and any fibres. Put into saucepan and cover with water. Add peppercorns, bay leaf, parsley and salt. Cover pan and poach gently, with the water

167

just simmering, for 20 minutes. Drain thoroughly and transfer to a warm serving-dish. Heat butter in a small pan until it turns a deep golden colour. Remove from heat and trickle in the vinegar (ignore the splutter!). Stir in capers then pour at once over brains. Serve straight away and accompany with creamed potatoes.

PISSALADIÈRE (Serves 8)

A Mediterranean onion-pie with all the flavour and all the colour one would expect from this southern sunspot. I ate my first Pissaladière (which was a small individual one) some years ago in a Menton street market, in between buying ripe figs for practically nothing a kilo and the sweetest melons on earth for 2d. each!

True Pissaladière is made with bread dough. But for speed I compromise and use pastry. I also use a flattish pizza tin from Italy for baking it in or else a large, 10-inch flan tin.

8 oz. short-crust pastry (pie pastry)	2 oz. canned anchovy fillets in oil
6 large onions (Spanish for choice)	2 tablespoons tomato *purée* salt and pepper to taste
4 tablespoons olive oil	16 large black olives
3 skinned and chopped tomatoes	

Roll out pastry thinly and use to line pizza tin or 10-inch flan tin. Line with aluminium foil to prevent pastry from rising as it cooks. Bake in centre of hot oven (425°F. or Gas No. 7) 20 minutes. Remove from oven and carefully lift out foil. Peel onions and cut into thin slices. Separate slices into rings. Heat oil in large saucepan. Add onions and cover pan. Fry over the gentlest possible heat for between ¾ to 1 hour, when onions should be very soft and almost thick in texture. Chop tomatoes and anchovies and add to onions with *purée*. Mix well then season to taste with salt and pepper. Transfer to flan case and stud with olives. Cook in centre of moderately hot oven (375°F. or Gas No. 5) for 20 minutes. Serve hot or cold.

POTATO PANCAKES (Serves 4 to 6)

Supposedly Jewish but claimed by Germans, Austrians and Poles as theirs too. But no matter. They are far too good to argue over and if you love potatoes and have no weight problems, make them next time instead of chips and serve them pan-hot, crisply golden and still sizzling.

1¼ lb. peeled and grated
  potatoes (approximately
  2 cups)
1 medium grated onion
  (approximately ½ cup)

2 tablespoons flour
2 eggs, beaten
  salt and pepper to taste
  oil for frying

Put potatoes and onion into bowl. Add flour, eggs and salt and pepper to taste. Mix well and leave, covered, for 30 minutes. (The mixture will turn an extraordinary muddy-brown colour but this has no effect whatsoever on flavour.) Heat about 1 inch of oil in a large frying-pan or skillet. Drop tablespoons of mixture into hot oil. Flatten with back of spoon and fry until crisp and golden on both sides, allowing about 2 minutes per side. Drain on paper towels and stack on a warm plate. Serve, Jewish style, with boiled salted brisket and pickled cucumbers or make the pancakes outsize and eat alone with apple sauce, for a cold weather snack, as they do in southern Germany.

BLANQUETTE OF LAMB (Serves 4)

Usually a blanquette is made with veal or chicken but, when in Denmark some years ago, I was pleasantly surprised to find this dish prepared with lamb. It was extremely good and made an interesting change from our classic roast lamb with mint sauce or Irish stew! One thing is very important though. The cut of meat must be as lean as lean can be (otherwise the blanquette would be very greasy), which is why I use lamb fillet.

1½ lb. lean fillet of lamb,
  cut from leg
½ pint water (1¼ cups)
½ pint milk (1¼ cups)
4 cloves
2 medium peeled onions
1 bay leaf
1 blade mace
1 level teaspoon salt
1 oz. butter or margarine
  (⅛ cup)

2 level tablespoons flour
4 oz. sliced mushrooms
  (1¼ cups)
  salt and pepper to taste
2 egg-yolks
1 tablespoon lemon juice
  about 1 lb. EACH freshly
  cooked green peas and small
  carrots

169

Cut lamb into 1-inch cubes. Put into saucepan with water. Bring to boil and remove scum. Pour in milk. Press cloves into onions, and add to pan with bay leaf, mace and salt. Bring slowly to boil and lower heat. Cover and simmer for about $1\frac{1}{4}$ hours or until lamb is tender. Strain liquor and reserve. Transfer meat to a warm platter or dish and keep hot. Melt butter or margarine in a saucepan. Stir in flour and cook 2 minutes without browning. Gradually blend in strained liquor. Cook, stirring, until mixture comes to boil and thickens. Add mushrooms and simmer 7 minutes. Adjust seasoning to taste and remove from heat. Beat egg-yolks and lemon juice well together. Combine with sauce and pour over lamb. Garnish edge of platter with alternate mounds of peas and carrots.

SWEET-SOUR PORK CHOPS (Serves 4)

1 medium chopped onion
($\frac{1}{2}$ cup)
1 oz. butter ($\frac{1}{8}$ cup)
2 level tablespoons cornflour
(corn starch)
$\frac{1}{4}$ pint wine vinegar ($\frac{2}{3}$ cup)
$\frac{1}{4}$ pint water ($\frac{2}{3}$ cup)

1 tablespoon soy sauce
2 tablespoons sugar
2 tablespoons chutney or
sweet pickle
salt to taste
4 pork chops, each about 6 oz.
melted butter

Fry onion slowly in the butter for 10 to 12 minutes or until pale gold. Stir in cornflour (corn starch) then gradually blend in vinegar, water and soy sauce. Cook, whisking continuously, until sauce comes to boil and thickens. Add sugar, chutney or pickle and salt to taste. Cover and simmer gently for 20 minutes. Meanwhile, cook chops. Stand in grill pan and brush with butter. Grill 7 to 10 minutes, depending on thickness. Turn over, brush with more melted butter and grill a further 7 to 10 minutes. Transfer to platter and coat with sauce. Accompany with freshly boiled noodles or rice and a green vegetable.

BŒUF À LA MODE (Serves 6)

A luxury French pot-roast.

3 lb. piece of chuck steak
1 cut garlic clove
  pepper
3 level tablespoons flour
3 tablespoons salad oil
¾ pint dry red wine (2 cups)
1 dozen shallots or small onions
6 carrots

1 small bay leaf
2 parsley sprigs
1 small calf's foot (if available)
1 liqueur glass brandy
  (optional)
2 to 3 level teaspoons salt
8 oz. sliced raw mushrooms
  (2½ cups)

Rub meat all over with cut clove of garlic, sprinkle lightly with pepper then cover with flour. Heat oil in large saucepan. Add meat and fry quickly on all sides. Pour wine into pan then add peeled shallots or onions, the whole, peeled carrots, bay leaf, parsley, calf's foot and brandy if used. Season with salt then bring very slowly to the boil. At once lower heat and cover pan. Simmer very gently for 3 hours. Add mushrooms and continue to cook slowly a further 30 minutes. Transfer meat to a large warm serving-dish, arrange vegetables round it then coat with gravy. Cut in slices to serve.

DEVILLED CHICKEN (Serves 4)

4 level tablespoons flour
1 level teaspoon salt
⅛ teaspoon cayenne pepper
4 joints roasting chicken
3 tablespoons salad oil
4 tablespoons boiling water
4 tablespoons tomato ketchup
2 tablespoons brown sugar
3 tablespoons wine vinegar

1 level teaspoon prepared
  mustard
2 teaspoons Worcestershire
  sauce
1 tablespoon lemon juice
1 medium chopped onion
  (½ cup)
1 oz. melted butter or
  margarine (⅛ cup)

Mix flour with salt and cayenne pepper. Use to coat chicken joints. Heat oil in large frying-pan or skillet. Add chicken (and any loose flour) and fry on both sides until crisp and golden. Combine all remaining ingredients well together. Pour into pan or skillet over chicken. Slowly bring to boil and lower heat. Cover and simmer 45 minutes to 1 hour or until chicken is tender. Serve with rice and a green vegetable.

WEST AFRICAN BANANA-STUFFED BEEF
(Serves 4 to 6)

1½ lb. rump steak, in one piece
    salt, pepper and dry mustard
    a little powdered nutmeg
2 bananas

juice of ½ a lemon
2 teaspoons sugar
4 bacon rashers

Cut a pocket in the steak and sprinkle with salt, pepper, mustard and nutmeg. Slice bananas thickly, toss in lemon juice, and pack into pocket with sugar. Join cut edges of meat together by sewing with thick thread. Stand in roasting tin. Cover with bacon rashers and bake in centre of moderately hot oven (400°F. or Gas No. 6) for 30 minutes. Serve cut in slices.

PINEAPPLE WITH CREAM AND CARAMEL ALMONDS (Serves 4)

4 large rings canned pineapple
2 level dessertspoons caster
    sugar
3 teaspoons butter
4 dessertspoons flaked almonds
3 dessertspoons pineapple syrup
    (from can)

3 teaspoons Kirsch or Grand
    Marnier
¼ pint double cream (⅔ cup
    whipping cream)
1 dessertspoon sifted icing sugar
    (confectioner's sugar)

Stand pineapple rings on 4 individual plates. Put caster sugar into a small pan. Stand over a low heat and stir until it melts and turns pale gold. Add butter, almonds and pineapple syrup and cook slowly, stirring, until the mixture turns a rich caramel colour. Remove from heat and gradually add liqueur. Beat cream and icing sugar together until thick. Pile equal amounts over pineapple rings then top with caramel and almond mixture. Serve straight away.

GALA FRUITS WITH ICE-CREAM (Serves 6)

6 heaped tablespoons finely
    chopped walnuts
6 level tablespoons chopped
    dates
6 macaroons, crumbled

1 dozen *glacé* cherries, chopped
6 tablespoons seedless raisins
6 tablespoons port
6 scoops vanilla ice-cream
6 wafer biscuits

Put equal amounts of walnuts, dates, macaroons, cherries and raisins into 6 wine or sundae glasses. Add a tablespoon of port to each. Cover and leave to stand for at least 1 hour at kitchen temperature. Just before serving, add a scoop of ice-cream to each and top with a wafer biscuit.

BANANA PUFFS (Makes about 8 to 12)

1 small packet frozen puff
pastry
apricot jam

4 medium sized bananas
sifted icing sugar
(confectioner's sugar)

Roll out pastry as directed on the packet and cut into 2-inch by 3-inch oblongs. Spread thinly with jam to within $\frac{1}{2}$ inch of edges. Cut bananas into 2-inch pieces and stand on pastry. Moisten edges with water then fold over like sausage rolls. Press edges well together to seal, then transfer to ungreased baking tray. Bake near top of hot oven (425°F. or Gas No. 7) for 12 to 15 minutes or until golden brown and well puffed. Remove from oven and dredge thickly with sifted icing (or confectioner's) sugar. Serve warm with whipped cream.

SHERRY COBBLER (Serves 6)

An old English summer drink.

Cover base of 6 tumblers with crushed ice, putting about 1 tablespoon into each with 1 slice of lemon and a fresh mint leaf. Half fill tumblers with sweet sherry then top up with chilled lemonade. Serve straight away with straws.